The Light on the Lord's Face

The LIGHT ON THE LORD'S FACE

J. WINSTON PEARCE

BROADMAN PRESS

Nashville, Tennessee

Quotations identified as NEB are from *The New English Bible,* ©
The Delegates of the Oxford University Press and the Syndics of the
Cambridge University Press, 1961. Quotations identified as Phillips are
from *The New Testament in Modern English,* © J. B. Phillips, 1958.
Used with permission of The Macmillan Company.

Library of Congress Catalog Card Number: 72–117298
Dewey Decimal Classification Number: 242
Printed in the United States of America
20.5 My 70 KSP

Dedicated to my nephew, Reverend Edwin Ray Frazier, whose countenance turns toward the "Light on the Lord's Face"

CONTENTS

1. The Light on the Lord's Face   9

2. The River and the Oak   18

3. "The Heart Is a Lonely Hunter"   26

4. "An 'De Walls Come Tumblin' Down"   35

5. My Favorite Things   43

6. Make No More Giants, God   53

7. What Are Your Boundaries?   61

8. Lantern in My Hand   69

9. Thank God a Man Can Grow   78

10. A Heart Fixed to Give   86

11. Home for Christmas (Christmas theme)   93

12. On Making Covenants (New Year's theme)   102

13. Mark the Earth with a Cross (Good Friday theme)   109

14. Lazarus Laughed (Easter theme)   118

15. "What's in a Name?"   124

1

"THE LIGHT ON THE LORD'S FACE"

Let us begin by recalling a delightful anecdote. It is the story of the little girl with paper and crayons. She sits on the floor drawing. Mother: "What are you drawing?" Child: "A picture of God." Mother: "But, dear, you can't draw a picture of God; no one knows what God looks like." Child: "They will when I get through."

There you have an intimation, an intimation of something that is as old as the human race. What is God like? We want to know. Is he friendly or is he hostile? In one of the oldest bits of writing in the Bible the cry is heard, "Oh that I knew where I might find him!" It was voiced by a disciple, "Show us the Father and we shall be satisfied."

The apostle Paul comes to grip with it. He says, "For the same God who said, 'Out of darkness let light shine,' has caused his light to shine within us, to give the light of revelation—the revelation of the glory of God in the face of Jesus Christ" (NEB). So, if we want to know what God is like we shall discover it in the light on the Lord's face. When the request and the affirmation were made, "Show us the Father and we shall be satisfied"; Jesus answered, "He who has seen me has seen the Father." Then, to see God look at Jesus Christ, for there, in the light on his face, we shall be able to discern God.

Let us at once be clear on this: Paul does not mean the physical face of Jesus. No one knows, even after all our childish drawings, what that face was like. We have our favorite artists and pictures. A certain amount of authority has been claimed for some of the pictures. Kahil Gibran, after he had completed his picture, "Jesus, the Son of Man," wrote to a friend saying, "This is his picture; I have seen him three times." But, Gibran's Jesus is not the Jesus that others have "seen." Let us not be wooden and unimaginative. Paul does not mean a physical face.

When the text says, "face," it means identity; it means person; it means Jesus Christ. The text uses a figure of speech by which the whole of a thing is put forth for a part, or a part for the whole. For example, we may speak of "bread" when we mean food; or we may speak of "army" when we mean a soldier; fifty "sails" may mean fifty ships. The technical word is synecdoche. The "light on the Lord's face" means the life, teachings, death, and resurrection of Christ the Lord. And, in that "light" what do we learn of God?

At once we learn the importance of faith. If it were possible, we may sometimes wish it were possible, to come to the gospels as if we had never come to them before, to read them as for the very first time, what would be the predominant impressions? Surely one of the firmest impressions would be this: "Have faith in God." That was his theme, his bugle note. He said, "According to your faith be it unto you." He said, "If you have faith as a grain of mustard seed"; "O woman, great is thy faith"; "I have not found so great a faith, no, not in Israel"; "O you of little faith, wherefore did you doubt?"; "Your faith hath made you whole"; "When the Son of Man comes will he find faith?" This was the note that he trumpeted so often and so insistently that we may well wonder if it would not be his primary word to us today.

Were he among us today, and he is; but, were he among us today so that with these physical eyes we could see him, and with these physical ears we could hear his voice, and if each were to go to him, as each would go to him, with his fears, failures, frustrations, and sins saying, "Master, what lack I yet?" Would he not say, "Have faith in God."

Might he not say, "You think your great problem is a pagan culture; you think it is strife and lawlessness in your streets, rebellion on your campuses; you think your problem is a break in the dam of morality that has held back the floods of sin and corruption for a thousand years, the breakup of homes, the chaos and anarchy in families. You think your problem is war and rumors of war with a threat of total annihilation. You believe your problem is inequality between races; you believe it is your inability to communicate with each other, a lack of deep caring on the part of the priviledged for the unpriviledged, the whole for the sick, the saved for the lost. You think it is an exploding population, a pollution of earth, air, and water."

"All this," I think he might say, "may be true enough, and tragic enough, but there is something more basic and fundamental. You do not have faith in God! And, until you have faith in God you begin at no beginning, and you move toward no ending. If you had faith in God all things would be possible for you; if you had faith in God you would be pleasing to God."

Now, this is not to say that faith equals magic, that faith is a sort of wand to wave over problems and, as in childhood fairy stories, the problems disappear. But great faith gives adequate motivation, helps choose appropriate methods, reveals proper evaluations, guarantees unfailing endurance, and adequate resources. And, without a great faith in God, none of these are vouchsafed to us.

If only in the light on the Lord's face each reader could make his own private confession of faith. Allow me to state mine, believing, when I do, that I shall be stating the faith heeded by many readers. To the best of my knowledge and experience these things I do believe, on these I stand, after these I do not place question marks, I place exclamation marks. I seek new light upon the implication and application of these affirmations, but as to their reality and their reliability, my heart is fixed. In affirming this faith I am not boastful, but I am bold, not in myself, but in the truth of this faith.

> I affirm the reality and the goodness of God; that for me is a closed issue.

I affirm the faithfulness and the trustworthiness of Jesus Christ, here I raise my voice and with the Psalmist cry, "My heart is fixed, O God."

I affirm the relevancy and the value of Holy Scriptures for instruction and the nurture of the Christian life. Here my "yes" is yes and my "no" is no.

I affirm the efficacy of prayer; like the man born blind, there may be, and there are, many things that I do not know but of a few things I am sure, one of these is the difference to my spiritual welfare that prayer makes.

I affirm the divine origin, the creative place, and continuing purpose of the church in the plan of God for the good of man.

I affirm the moral quality of this universe; the scales are weighted on the side of righteousness.

I acknowledge my personal responsibility for making this faith known; I admit that I am a debtor.

When Henry David Thoreau was a boy someone asked what he was going to be when he became a man. The man in the boy answered: "I shall be unanimous." If we could only be "unanimous" on some such affirmation of faith today! I do not plead for just an intellectualizing of such a faith. I plead for the incarnation of that faith. I ask that such a faith be given a body in which to live and move and have its being, to the end that such faith may be brought to bear upon the world in which we live. Such a faith is seen in the light on the Lord's face.

Look again. In the light on the Lord's face we may see a great joy and gladness. We followers of the Christ have all but forgotten that truth. We have emphasized another portrait, the portrait of grief and sorrow. We sing in the Philip Bliss hymn, "Man of sorrows what a name for the Son of God who came." The Prophet Isaiah's words have become our favorite portrait,

But he was wounded for our transgressions, he was bruised for our iniquities: the chastisement of our peace was upon him; and with his stripes we are healed. . . . He was oppressed and he was afflicted, yet he opened not his mouth: he is brought as a lamb to the slaughter, and as a sheep before her shearers is dumb, so he opened not his mouth.

These are legitimate and true pictures, but they are not the only true and legitimate pictures. We must not forget that it was "for the joy that was set before him that he endured the cross," and thought nothing of its shame. The fourth Gospel records the words of Jesus, "These things have I spoken unto you, that my joy might remain in you, and that your joy might be full." He wanted his followers to have courage for he had overcome the world.

If the gospels could be read with no preconceived notions and impressions and prejudices, probably one of the dominant impressions received would be that Jesus was a well-adjusted, harmonious, happy, and triumphant spirit. We would see that he delighted in feasts, relished banquets, and rejoiced in social conversation. A recent cartoon shows a tired business tycoon at his big mahogany desk. He presses the call button for his secretary; he tells her that he is lonely. She is to get him a gifted conversationalist. So much of life is like that, except we cannot demand "gifted conversationalists."

Again and again the gospels tell us that Jesus went into a house to eat, that it came to pass as he sat at meat, that they made for him a banquet, that there was a feast and Jesus and his disciples were there. Now, feasting was an oriental custom; often there was music and dancing. The people mingled their eating with feasting and their feasting was celebration. It has been said that for much of his public ministry Jesus was "society's most sought after dinner guest." The straight laced said that he was too gay to be good; he was too happy to be holy. It was this side of his life that brought some of the severest criticism.

His popularity was amazing. The crowds pressed him so there was no time for him to eat. They "thronged him" in the streets; they crowded him on the shore; the multitudes followed him great distances making it impossible for him to find seclusion.

Women ministered to him; children were given into his arms that he might bless them; other children crowded about him and were used as object lessons.

His teachings were no less exciting than his life. When he told a story there was color, movement, and drama: banquets, harvests, treasure hunts, kings setting out to battle, hypocrites on parade, demons on the warpath, weddings and celebrations. He called himself the "bridegroom"; he said the kingdom that he came to establish was like a wedding. He began his work, according to John, by attending a wedding, and he closed it by going on a fishing trip with his disciples and cooking breakfast for them!

Think if you will what that kind of spirit must have meant in that day to the poor, the tired, the lonely, the frustrated, the hopeless, the bored. Think of what such a spirit would mean to the tired, the frustrated, the hopeless ones today.

A prominent physician said to his minister that the most deadly disease from which his patients suffered was one that his medicine could not reach nor his knife remove. "Cancer?" asked the minister. "No," replied the physician. "We shall one day be able to deal effectively with cancer. The disease of which I speak," the doctor continued, "is boredom. It is our worst enemy. For it is not only deadly in itself, it is also the cause of other deadly problems such as gambling, drinking, immorality, and death itself. The reason many people die is not that they have a reason for dying but that they have no reason for living."

Many of the early followers of Jesus caught something of his joyous spirit. They sang in prison and amidst earthquakes, they rejoiced as the caskets of their loved ones were lowered in the grave; they lifted their voices in shouts of thanksgiving as the wild beasts rushed upon them in the arenas and as the fires snuffed out their breath they sang their doxologies. No wonder people stormed the church doors, tried to bribe and buy the secret of this joy and triumph!

The little Salvation Army lass had been rescued from the

lower depths of crime and the gutters. She loved music and was placed in the band. But her loud blasts on the trumpet made it impossible for any other instrument in the band to be heard. The conductor spoke to her; she promised to ease up on the volume, but soon she was back at it again; the volume of her instrument was drowning out everyone else. Again the conductor spoke to her, and then she said: "I am sorry; it is not that I do not want to be a member of the band and cooperate in all that you ask me to do. It is just that when I remember what the Lord Jesus Christ has done for me I could blow this . . . old horn straight!" One need not approve the adjective to hail the spirit of enthusiasm and joy. And, it may be, that even the adjective is more acceptable than the mood and spirit of pessimism that pervades so much of our Christianity. "Joy," said Gilbert Chesterton, "is the gigantic secret of the Christian." The prophet Isaiah said, "Ye shall go out with joy, and be led forth with peace: the mountains and hills shall break forth before you into singing, and all the trees of the fields shall clap their hands." By the light on the Lord's face it is possible to discern a great joy and gladness.

See further in the light on the Lord's face a life directing purpose. Jesus was not idle while he was here among men. He knew a great joy; he knew no idleness: he was not rudderless. He knew why he was here; he knew where he was going when his task was over. One of the many dramatic scenes in those last hours that Jesus had with his disciples shows how he arose from the table, knowing full well that God had given all things into his hands. Knowing that he had come from God and that he was going to God, he laid aside his garments and took a towel. There it is. He knew his task; he knew from whence he came; he knew where he was going, in order to do his work, "He took a towel."

That purpose and mission all but consumed him. He said, "I have a baptism to be baptized with; and how I am constrained until it is accomplished!" He said, "I came . . . not to do my own will, but the will of him who sent me." And, again he said, "The son of man came not to be ministered unto, but to minister, and to give his life a ransom for many."

Now, the disciple may not forget his own mission, for he does have one. Those early disciples were told that as God had sent Christ, just so they were being sent by Christ. Dwight L. Moody said, "A Christian is someone to whom God entrusts all his fellowmen." And William James affirmed, "The greatest use of life is to spend it for something that will outlast it."

The early disciples were caught up in that. It became a source of the great joy that they knew and helps explain the great things that they did. Looking at those men, as they were when Christ found them, who would believe that they could become and that they could do the things that they became and did. Who, by the wildest stretch of vision and scheme could see them "turning the world upside down," and becoming, as they did become, and being known, as they have been known for nearly two thousand years, "The glorious company of the apostles!" Imagine that being said of vacillating Peter, of thunderous John, of silent Andrew, of doubting Thomas, and of those in that little band of whom the writers of the New Testament did not even feel led to list their names after Jesus called them.

But they came to feel that they were possessed by a great purpose and that resources had been promised for the accomplishing of that purpose—and nothing and no one could stop them.

From their day to ours, here and there and yonder, a few men and women, never a large number in any one generation nor in any one part of the world, but a few individuals have been so possessed by such an overpowering purpose and mission. When these individuals have come to birth the world has had to take notice and to make way for them, their mission and work.

To see that phenomenon is one of the great experiences of life. The world is seldom so profoundly moved as when it sees an individual or a small group of individuals, so possessed.

When such a man comes along cynics, skeptics, scoffers, nihilists, sophisticates, tired do-gooders, the hard and the crusty all are ready, if not to cheer, at least to salute. This is true even in the entertainment field. Who would think that in these times a tired, jaded, cynical, frustrated, modern audience could be moved, as they have been moved, by a song like "The Impossible Dream" from *A Man of La Mancha?* Yet, it sometimes brings a crowd to its feet, sometimes copious tears flow, always a lump rises in the throat, as the song rolls over the audience with its challenge of idealism, purpose, mission, and daring.

2

"THE RIVER AND THE OAK"

Elizabeth Yates begins her inspiring story of *Howard Thurman, Portrait of a Practical Dreamer* by saying that there was a river and there was an oak in the life of the young Howard Thurman.

These seemed to bind the world of the young Negro boy. He was eleven then, and lived in Daytona, Florida. He had gone to school and had completed the seventh grade; that was as far as he could go; it was as far as any Negro in Daytona had ever gone in school.

His life was restricted physically, socially, intellectually, and, to a lesser degree, spiritually. The Negro settlement was closely hedged. He could not, for example, leave the Negro settlement and cross the river at night without a letter of authorization signed by a white man.

But, there was the river and there was the oak. The river flowed within sight of his home. The oak was in his yard. On the river his thoughts roamed far; horizons lifted; imagination knew no bounds. In the oak his thoughts found a haven; his dreams were saddled; his imagination bit into reality. One stretched him, the other disciplined him. Both were necessary to his growing.

Years later, May 25, 1963, Howard Thurman returned to Daytona to give the Baccalaureate Address at Bethune-Cookman College. He was a world citizen now. Educational institutions throughout the land had honored themselves when they had honored him in bestowing honorary degrees. He was now Minister-at-Large of Boston University; formerly Dean of Marsch Chapel, Boston University; Dean of Rankin Chapel,

Howard University; Cofounder and Minister Emeritus, Church for the Fellowship of All People, San Francisco; Fellow, National Council of Religion in Higher Education and American Academy of Arts and Sciences; author of books and articles in learned journals, contributor to the *Interpreter's Bible,* friend and confidant of the world's great.

Daytona was glad now to do him honor. The day was designated "Howard Thurman Day," throughout the city. The mayor met him; read a proclamation that made Howard Thurman an honorary citizen of the city. A key to the city was presented to him. The car that carried him, his family, and the mayor was followed by a motorcade of city officials and friends. There followed four marching bands. The streets were lined with crowds: watching, waving, cheering.

Following the Baccalaureate Address there was a reception. Old and young, great and less great, black and white, men, women, and children, old friends, young friends, new friends, and those who eagerly wished to be friends, were present.

Among the old friends was Howard Thurman's kindergarten teacher of fifty-eight years gone by. Once she seemed very big, now she seemed very small. But when she looked at him he felt again the power of those eyes that had first challenged him to work with that within himself which had nothing to do with color or surrounding circumstances.

Following the reception he went to the home of the old doctor, now retired and feeble, who more than a half-century before had befriended and encouraged him, had given him a pair of shoes and advised him to learn to wear them for, "You've got a long way to go." At the old doctor's request Howard Thurman knelt by the chair and prayed.

When all the "shouting and the tumult" had died away, Dr. Thurman took his family and sought out his old oak tree. He told them what the tree had meant to him as a small and growing boy. He told them that when he was a boy it did not matter what happened to him, disappointment, heartache, frus-

tration, anger, humiliation, if he could just get his back against
the oak tree, if he could just feel its rugged bark with his hands,
he was steadied. Against its great trunk he could believe there
were some things that were dependable and durable.

Then he took his family down to the river, the river where he
had fished and rowed and dreamed. As the oak had anchored
him; so, the river had kept him moving. The river was like life
he said. "It is the nature of a river to flow, to keep always
flowing. Nothing can stop it. Lives as well as rivers have their
flood times. Crises may come that will shift the river to another
channel or enlarge its course as it moves to an ultimate goal, but
nothing can stop its onward flowing. *Nothing.*" [1] And, as long as
a man has a dream in his heart, he cannot lose the significance
of living.

There the man of sixty joined the boy of six in gratitude for
the river and the oak. One gave exposure, the other gave
enclosure; one gave discipline, the other gave liberty; one spoke
of local loyalties, the other emphasized social obligations. These
are the ins and the outs of life; these are the comings and the
goings, the tarryings and the travelings, the waitings and the
wanderings, field and fold, here and now, there and then.

The emphasis is a biblical one. The psalmist said, "The Lord
shall preserve thy going out and thy coming in from this time
forth, and even for evermore." Jesus declared, "I am the door:
by me if any man enter in, he shall be saved, and shall go in and
out, and find pasture." Chase that truth out in several different
directions and you will see its relevancy.

Immediately you think of the oak of enclosure and the river
of exposure of the Christian faith. No man is prepared to expose
his faith to men until that faith has been enclosed in communion
and fellowship with God. Recently the *Saturday Review* had a
cartoon showing two characters sitting by the garbage can; even
in that sad state their features marked them as men who had
known better days. One was saying to the other, "I was so busy
trying to save the world that I forgot about me." There had

been exposure without enclosure and the results were tragic. They always are.

Of course, this position violates today's "sacred cows." Today a man is criticized for any form of faith's enclosure. This, we are assured is a protective measure that is totally unworthy of a man who would call himself Christian; it is a form of escape, a totally selfish act, a concern for self at the expense of others.

Now, there is an element of truth in the accusation. The enclosure of faith is a protective measure, it is a form of escape. But, it is the protection of the fort on the frontier that shields the settlers from angry enemies while reinforcements are summoned and while the cavalry is reequipped. It is the safety of the harbor while the ship is being reconditioned and fresh supplies are being taken aboard. It is the escape of sleep that "knitteth up the raveled sleeve of care."

This kind of escape is absolutely essential to all worthy living. The Scriptures are not slow to affirm it. "Thou preparest a table before me in the presence of mine enemies: thou anointest my head with oil; my cup runneth over." And, who will claim that as an example of selfishness! "He is my refuge and my fortress." Escape? "Come unto me," said Jesus, "and I will give you rest." Protection?

Or, turn to the hymns of faith. Among those that are best loved because they have spoken most meaningfully to life are hymns that recognize this note of "enclosure." "Rock of ages, cleft for me; Let me hide myself in thee." Remember "Jesus, lover of my soul, Let me to thy bosom fly." Or, "Come ye disconsolate, where'er ye languish, Come to the mercy seat, fervently kneel; Here bring your wounded hearts, here tell your anguish: Earth has no sorrow that hea'vn cannot heal." Any one who does not recognize the need and the relevancy of that note in the experiences of life has never known life. This is the enclosure of faith.

But, forget not that enclosure must lead to exposure. Indeed, one of the main, if not the main, purpose of faith's enclosure is to the end that it may be exposed. The window of faith must be open "toward Jerusalem," but the door of faith must open onto the streets of the world. "Happy art thou, O Israel: who is like unto thee, O people saved by the Lord, the shield of thy help (enclosure), the sword of thy excellency" (exposure). A harbor from the storms, yes; but, a harbor is not just a place into which ships flee for protection from storms; it is, also, a place from which ships go forth to do business in great waters in spite of the storms, at times because of storms.

"Come unto me and I will give you rest," said the Master of life, but do not stop there, "Take my yoke upon you, and learn of me." "Yokes?" exposure. Remember the little verse that speaks of people who live within the sound of church and chapel bell, but the author would like to run a rescue shop within a mile of hell? No exposure without enclosure preceeding it; no enclosure without exposure following it.

There follows this implication, the oak of discipline and the river of freedom, the coming ins of discipline and the going outs of freedom. Our age is not characterized by its discipline. Up in the Smoky Mountains there was a political gathering on the courthouse square. Old Zeek was shouting himself hoarse as the political spellbinder held forth. Between the peaks of excitement a friend nudged Zeek and said, "Zeek, tell me, what do you really think of this speaker?" Zeek shouted his answer, "I didn't come here to think; I came here to holler."

There are a number of ways that the "Now Generation," and the "Go-Go" groups may be pegged; disciplined people they are not. There may be, I think there are, some assets on their side. Orderliness, control, respect for heritage and tradition are not. One of the basic reasons for this is their philosophy. Theirs is the position that the only way to know about a thing is to experience it yourself; to know it, you have to do it. That position is both unwise and dangerous.

One of the basic assumptions of all civilized life is that you do not have to do everything over from the beginning. It is possible for men to see, experience, think, meditate, work, use the crucible of life, write on stones, parchment, books, monuments, structure knowledge into laws, constitutions, forms of government, and institutions. This accumulated wisdom becomes capital for future generations; it is possible for children's children to profit from much of this, to use quantities of it; they do not have to begin with scratch. It needs to be remembered that if you have no change you know no progress, but if you have no traditions you experience no civilization.

It is impossible to have one without the other. When the two are seen going hand in hand you observe the finest things that life can afford. A friend of mine was surprised and humbled when his mother's will was read. There was a large family; it was a closely knit family. But, when the will was read, this is what it said: "I leave everything I possess to my son Blank, to do with as he pleases, because he always pleases to do right." There is the river of freedom: "I leave everything I possess to my son . . . to do with as he pleases." But, do not forget the oak of discipline from which the freedom issued: "Because he always pleases to do right." No oak of discipline; no river of freedom. Remember the apostle Paul's statement, "The glorious liberty of the children of God." The way to life is straight and the gate is narrow; we have it on good authority that route is not crowded, but the Master insisted on telling it as it is.

Run this implication out in another direction and see the oak of local loyalties and the river of social concern. Kierkegaard once said that he asked the philosopher Hegel for a street address in Copenhagen and that Hegel gave him a map of Europe. And there is the story of the janitor who was cleaning in a bank. It was after bank hours; the janitor was alone. The telephone rang and he answered it, saying, "Hello; this is the First National Bank." The voice on the phone said, "I want to know what the Federal Reserve discount is, what the prime paper rate is, and if all this foreign travel is going to upset the currency." Five seconds of silence, then the voice of the janitor, "When I said, 'hello,' and 'this is the First National Bank,' I told you all I know about banking." Local addresses are important; knowledge of what local institutions are and what they do is essential.

Before we spend all of our time in trying to improve the world, let us spend a little time in trying to improve ourselves. We need to know and obey a few local ordinances before we try to rewrite the constitution of the world. We try to be the keeper of everyone else's vineyard, but our own vineyards we do not keep. The fact that we do not know our own children is scarcely the best recommendation for instructing the families of the world about their children. And, surely, a man needs to give some thought to his own relationship to Christ before he tries to convert the world, to give some attention to one local church before he sets forth to build and reform the churches of the world. Forget not, neglect not, despise not the oak of local loyalty.

Once a man has seen to his local loyalties his task is not finished; his task is beginning. For there are social causes, community, national, and world causes that claim his "ounce of courage." Many years ago Edmund Burke wrote, "All that is needed for the success of evil is that good people do nothing." It is still true. And those who have firm rootage in local loyalties are the people to care redemptively about social issues.

At midway of this century, E. M. House wrote a book called, *Saints In Politics*. It is the dramatic story of a small group of British politicians at the turn of the eighteenth century, Thomas Babington, Henry Thornton, William Wilberforce, and others. These were religious men. They were ardently evangelical in their faith. Their personal religion was the fountain spring of their social concern. They were, as Wilberforce himself said, ". . . true Christians who knew what it was to practice saintliness in daily life and by whom the minutest details of action were considered with reference to eternity." There is scarcely a moral, social, political, or religious reform in nineteenth century England that cannot be traced to the influence of these men. These men had their local, personal loyalties; these were their oaks; this was their "coming ins." But, they did not stop there. With John Wesley they said, "The world is our parish."

No follower of Christ can afford to be indifferent to the needs of the world, to the rivers of social condition that flow from his door out to the far places of the earth. The emphasis of the New Testament is emphatic about that: "The devil showed him all the kingdoms of the *world*." "I am the light of the *world*." "The field is the *world*"; "The gospel shall be preached in all the *world*"; "The lamb of God that taketh away the sin of the *world*"; "God so loved the *world*."

There was a river and there was an oak. There is a promise, "The Lord shall preserve thy going out and thy coming in from this time forth, and even for evermore." There is a condition, "I am the door," said Jesus, "by me if any man enter in, he shall be saved, and shall go in and out, and find pasture."

NOTES

1. Yates, Elizabeth. *Howard Thurman, Portrait of a Practical Dreamer,* The John Day Company, 1964, p. 218.

3

"THE HEART
IS A LONELY HUNTER"

"My heart," wrote William Sharp, "is a lonely hunter that hunts on a lonely hill." Carson McCullers thought enough of that haunting confession to make it the title of her popular novel. Motion picture executives thought enough of the novel to make it into a beautiful, if not disturbing, picture.

"The heart is a lonely hunter that hunts on a lonely hill." Right! It is and it does. The best loved short story in the world, the parable of the prodigal son, emphasizes the truth.

Consider the hunter and his rebellion. Man is a hunter. All men are hunters. All men have always been hunters. They have not hunted in the same way; they do not always hunt for the same game. Nor, do they hunt for different game on the same hills, but man is, and always has been a hunter. Columbus hunts for a sea route. Galileo hunts for a planet. The biologist hunts for a death dealing germ. The astronauts hunt for the moon. All men hunt for happiness and God.

This is one of the basic truths of the story of the prodigal son. He was a hunter. He wanted something, something he did not think he possessed, nor did he believe it could be had on the "hill" where he had been hunting, his home. So he became impatient, restless, and rebellious. He was determined to hunt elsewhere, to live his own life, in his own way, on his own chosen hills. In doing this he rejected his home, parental discipline, accepted social customs, and all old loyalties. He sought new friends, a new set of social and ethical standards. The "establishment," the "power structure," the "old morality," as he had known them were left behind. He became a rebel, but the thing that made him rebel was his hunting instinct. He believed he could find what he wanted if he hunted for it in the right place; and the right place, was anywhere except where he was, doing what he was doing, encountering what he was then experiencing.

Run that fact out; run it out as far as you wish. You will see that young man's hunting instinct written large. You will find it exemplified in the intellectuals on college campuses, in the minorities of the urban ghettos, in the hippies in their Haight Ashburys, the restless, rising, rebelling nations of the world. There may be "professionals" who wish, and do encourage and use this hunting instinct for their own purposes, but the "professionals" do not have to instill the desire for change, they only profit by what is already present. Carl Sandburg said, "God must have wanted man to be a changer. Else God wouldn't have put that awful unrest in him." So, you have it: the hunter going "into a far country" hunting for what he believes he can never find where he is.

Take another step, look at the hill and its difficulties. The "lonely hunter" goes hunting "on a lonely hill." It is that. The prodigal in the ancient story found it so. The modern day prodigals find it no less so. The hills are hard. The ancient prodigal spent his substance in riotous living. He spent "all;" he held nothing back. He was determined to find what he craved, though he was not quite sure what that was.

"And when he had spent all . . ." spent all his substance, all inheritance, all resources: time, energy, wealth, health, status, and statue, he was still aware of his "want." The hunter was still unsatisfied. His desire, instead of being lessened was multiplied and intensified. He "hired" himself out. He took the lowest possible form of employment. His case was so desperate that he sunk until his desires were the same as the hogs that were his companions. But, no one came to his aid. The hills were hard, difficult, friendless, brutalizing. He "spent all," all was now gone; pride, self-respect, dignity, decency.

Notice, the hills where he hunted were not only hard, they were futile. There is a dual purpose that prompts hunters to leave home. One is to seek what they believe it is impossible to find at home; the other is to escape what they do have at home. The hunter wants to get away from the influence of home, the discipline of the father. He wants to "live his own life," without laws and restraints.

But that is impossible; it always has been impossible. The psalmist could have told him. There is no place the prodigal can go where the Father is not. If he ascends up into heaven, the Father is there; if he makes his bed in hell, the Father is there. If he takes the wings of the morning and flies to the far corners, the Father will be present.

A truth that prodigals are slow to learn is this: one does not avoid the Father's discipline by fleeing, by ignoring, or by rebelling. The prodigals may choose the form of the love and discipline that the Father extends, but escape it? Never! One does not escape the laws of health by ignoring them or by denying their existence. Our crowded hospitals, sanatoriums, clinics, doctor's offices, psychiatrist couches, and prisons may, and often do, demonstrate the existence of the laws of health; they never prove that the laws of health are nonexistent, or that people avoid those laws by denying their existence or seeking to evade them by hunting on other hills.

It would be as easy to avoid the law of gravity or of logic by affirming that they did not exist in a "foreign country" as to avoid the Father by the same means. The prophet Amos said that the ever present God might be likened unto the experience of a man fleeing from a lion and meeting a bear, or of a man fleeing to his home, falling against the wall in exhaustion and a serpent, coiled and waiting, striking deep with his fangs.

The form of the "presence" and the discipline of the Father may be chosen. The reality of the presence and discipline cannot be avoided.

Emerson knew that; he said:

> The dice of God are always loaded;
> Every secret is told,
> Every crime is punished,
> Every wrong is redressed in silence
> And in certainty,
> The thief steals from himself;
> The swindler swindles from himself.

History and tradition are just as emphatic. There is a story of the Roman Emperor Julian, known as the Apostate Emperor. In childhood Julian had a friend by the name of Agathon. Their ways parted. Agathon became a Christian; Julian became a persecuting emperor. One day the two met, face to face. The emperor said, "Tell me, Agathon, what has become of the carpenter of Nazareth?" Pointing across the way where the multitudes were entering the pagan temple, he continued: "Has your carpenter any work these days? Are there still some small jobs coming his way?" Agathon, the Christian looked at his boyhood friend, now persecutor of the followers of the Nazareth carpenter and he said: "Yes, Julian, the carpenter of Nazareth is very busy these days. He is nailing together a coffin to put your empire in."

Well, if you know your history, you will remember that Julian's reign lasted less than two years. He was slain in battle with the Persians. And tradition has it, that as he fell, mortally wounded, he cried, "Galilean, thou hast conquered!"

Tradition? Possibly. But, hear this. "Be not deceived; God is not mocked: for whatsoever a man soweth, that shall he also reap." Someone has said that a free translation of that verse might be, "Don't kid yourself; you can't get away with it!" For, "Every plant," said Jesus, "which my heavenly Father hath not planted, shall be rooted up."

Of course, the matter of time is involved. You must not expect God to balance his books, nor ours, every Saturday night. This points up a major difference between the man of faith and the man of no faith. The man who has no faith in the

Father has to be concerned with time; time is all that he has. He must watch the clock and the calendar. What he does must be done quickly. He is a member of the "Now" generation. So, he takes the cash and lets the credit go, nor heeds the rumble of distant drums. But the men of faith are not bound by calendars and clocks. They can wait.

Pause for station identification: "The heart is a lonely hunter that hunts on a lonely hill." We have looked at the hunter and his rebellion, at the hill and its difficulties, now take another step, look at the heart and its loneliness.

No matter where the prodigal went, no matter what he did, no matter with whom he associated, no matter how dirty he became, no matter how long and unkept his hair and beard, no matter how many dissident groups he identified with, no matter how many "trips" he took by means of pot, or its first-century equivalent, he still remembered home and his father. And this is one of the significant things about the story; the young man remembered and was lonely.

"But," says the story, "when he came to himself." Then! Then he was not himself when he was rebelling and running, when he was hunting on the wrong hills for unworthy game. So, we are faced with the old and treasured word of Augustine again, "Thou hast made us for thyself and our hearts are restless until they find their rest in thee." God made man, and God left his thumb mark on him. One of the signs of that thumbprint is man's restless search for meaning and for identity; his heart is lonely.

Man is too great and noble to be satisfied with that which satisfies the mere animal. His heart is lonely until it finds its rest in the Father's house, feasting at the Father's table, responding to the Father's love. That is not a new discovery. Let the old Hebrew prophet say it:

Ho, every one that thirsteth, come ye to the waters, and he that hath no money; come ye, buy, and eat; yea, come, buy wine and milk without money and without price. Wherefore do you spend your money for that which is not bread? and your labour for that which satisfieth not? Harken diligently unto me, and eat ye that which is good, and let your soul delight itself in fatness. Incline your ear and come unto me: hear, and your soul shall live.

The myth makers had a story about the god of the sea in pursuit of a mortal. The man escaped from the sea just in time to elude the sea god's grasp. But, as the man raced up the shore a small wave was thrown into his heart. A smile came upon the sea god's face and he said, "The man will return to me; the sea is in his heart. He will ever be lonely and restless until he returns."

The ancients felt the loneliness of the heart but so do moderns. James Hilton gave voice to it in his novel, *Random Harvest*. It is the story of Charles Rainier, a man who was shell shocked in war and suffered amnesia from the experience. He was taken prisoner by the enemy. When Rainier regained awareness he was back in his native England. He did not know how he got back; he did not know who he was. It was as if his past had been lifted from him. He found his family, completed his university education, took his place in the family's vast business. He was successful. He became head of the business. He was elected to Parliament. He married. His wife was charming, devoted, and efficient. Her name was Helen. There was harmony between them, but they were never close to each other.

His heart was lonely. The past haunted him; he could not grasp it; it would not release him. Gradually his memory began to return, small bits of it. He never spoke of this to his wife, Helen. But he did begin to remember. And, he remembered that there had been a former marriage. The girl's name was Paula. That marriage to Paula, he now remembered, had been a completely happy one. Where was she now? Where was Paula? Was she alive? What was she doing? Had she remarried? Was she, somewhere, waiting for him?

One close friend who knew of Rainier's returning memory

strongly advised him to leave the past alone. The past presented problems. If Paula, his former wife, were alive she could have, had she desired, contacted him. He was famous; his name was constantly in the news. If he did find her there would be business and political complications, a famous man with two living wives. Besides, it would be unfair to Helen, his present wife; think of what it would mean to her. But, Rainier simply could not leave the past alone; it haunted him; he longed for it; he simply had to find Paula.

And, find her he did.

It came on a shining morning when drawn as by a magnet he walked from his office, never even bothering to cancel speaking engagements. He drove to a little town, drove to it as unerringly as a homing pigeon returns to its rest. He parked his car and began to climb. Then he found the place, two small windswept hills and nestling between, as though it were a saddle, a little lake. It was here he remembered that he and Paula declared their love; it was here that they had ceased to be two persons and had become one person. He fell to the ground, closed his eyes, and gave himself over to memory. And then she came to him. Paula, his lost love. For she too had been drawn to the spot. They stood for a moment looking into each other's eyes; then, they were in each other's arms. They were reunited, never to be parted again.

And Helen, his present wife? No problem. You see, Helen and Paula were one and the same person. Years before, while in his state of amnesia, Paula had found him, realized his condition. She changed her name, led him to depend upon her, to marry her. Always her heart longed to tell him who she really was, longed to tell him who he really was, longed to tell him what they were together. Yet, she knew that he would have to discover this for himself. So, she waited patiently and hopefully. Now, he had come to himself and in coming to himself, he had returned to her.

And, the Scriptures declare it: *When he came to himself* he said I will arise and go to my father." For the "heart is a lonely hunter that hunts on a lonely hill."

Another step must be taken. Consider home and the father's heart. The story is very clear, and very kind at this point. It says that when the father saw him, the hunter, his heart went out to him; the father ran, embraced his son, welcomed him, rejoiced over his return, celebrated the son's homecoming.

This point is not only necessary to the story; it is necessary to the gospel. For, you see, the gospel means "good news." And up to this point the story has been only "bad news." The story tells of the rebellious hunter; it tells of the hard and futile hills upon which he hunted; it tells of the lonely and hungry heart that could not find rest and meaning on any of those hunts and hills. Suppose that was all of the story—and—it is all of the story for multitudes of individuals. But, it is not all of the gospel. It is only the prologue to the gospel. There are the Father's house and the Father's heart.

This is not only the turning point of a great story, this throws light upon every other part of the story. It now becomes clear, with this last addition, that the parts of the story that at first seemed "bad news" are actually a part of the "good news." What if the hills upon which the son hunted had not been hard and futile? What if the heart had not been lonely? What if the hunter could have found peace, meaning and purpose on the lonely hills and among the pods and the pigs? Had his soul been only big enough to find completion in that the story would in truth be "bad news."

Now it can be seen that the father did not remain at home with no care or concern of love until the hunter came to himself. The Father and the Father's love never left the hunter. The Father was responsible for the hardness and the futility of the hills; the Father was responsible for the greatness and the loneliness of the heart. The Father used these as agents to assist in bringing the hunter "to himself," and to saying, "I will arise and go to my Father."

For this is the way life is. God does not stand, as the drama *Green Pastures* pictures him, at the window of heaven in anger hurling thunderbolts of hardness, trouble, and tragedy until the hunters are broken and forced home. But, the Father who created the world created man to enjoy the world, and created the world to be enjoyed by man. Not only do man and God belong together, man and the world belong to each other, but both belong within the will and purpose of the Father Creator. Neither life nor the world responds favorably apart from the will and purpose of God. "All things betray thee, who betrayest me." Did not the apostle Paul declare, "The whole created universe groans in all its parts as if in pangs of childbirth"? Poets as well as prophets have seen that.

And he came! So, as the poet would have it, after last returned the first, though a wide compass round was fetched— the restless hunter, the hard hills, the lonely heart, and the kind Father. Jesus told the story; the story is true, for in him is no darkness at all. The sailor comes home from the sea and the hunter is home from the hill. And there is great rejoicing over one sinner that repents.

4

"AN 'DE WALLS COME TUMBLIN' DOWN"

After more than four hundred years of slavery in Egypt the Israelites were led out of bondage by Moses. Moses was eighty years old; this was the crowning achievement of his life. It was as if everything that Moses had experienced and known before was preparation and prologue, a sort of marking time, waiting for the great moment, the moment of liberation. His studies in the universities of Egypt, his hot-headed outbursts of temper in the brickyards, tending sheep at the backside of the desert, listening for God's voice in the stillness, treading the narrow, winding mountain paths of Midian, waiting, always waiting in expectancy, for his giant hour, the hour when it would be right and wise to strike for liberty and independence.

The hour arrived. He received his orders. He went to Egypt. He faced the Pharaoh. He organized the Hebrews and led them out of Egypt, across the Red Sea, on into the desert, on toward the Promised Land. He did it. But, he was eighty years old; his strength was not as it had once been. His nerves were taut; his patience was worn thin, and he did not always give God the glory due him. So, God allowed Moses to get in sight of the Promised Land but would not allow him to enter it.

Moses was not the last military leader who had the ability to break the shackles of slavery but was unable to forge the bonds of freedom, to lead the people from bondage but not into liberty, to throw off one yoke but not put on another, the ability to break but not to build.

So, the Hebrews, a ragged, impatient, petulant group of people who have wandered for forty years in the wilderness now lose their leader. Moses dies; the angels bury him; no man knows his grave to this day. Moses' successor is chosen, he is Joshua, the son of Nun. This man Joshua is energetic, resourceful, and courageous. He has an almost uncanny sense of timing, and he is masterful in the realm of morale.

The way ahead is carefully studied. Reports from earth and heaven are received; secret meetings of the official command are held. A plan is agreed upon, and the people are informed. Early the next morning the people come to a marching position, silently they begin to march around the city of Jericho, easily in sight of the city but carefully out of weapon range; they march, march, silently march around the city.

It is not difficult to imagine conditions on the inside of the city's walls. For Jericho is prepared for battle. Its heavy guns are in place; eager soldiers man the battle stations. While round the city the Hebrews march. At first there is question and wonder on the part of the inhabitants of Jericho, then amazement, then smiles, then wild laughter: "These crazy Hebrews! Do they think that marching around the walls of our city will cause those walls to fall!" The Hebrews march and march and march, no conversation, no commands, just marching.

This procedure continued for six days—into camp at night, up and marching early in the morning. Round and round the city, march, march, no sound but the swishing of sandals on the burning desert sands, while the inhabitants watch from the walls of Jericho. But, on the seventh day there is excitement in the camp of the Hebrews. They line up for their march with added enthusiasm and purpose. As they begin to march the pace quickens until they are all but running, for today they are to go around the city seven times.

Then, a crisp, crackling, shrill order is given: "Halt!" "Attention!" The priests lift the trumpets to their lips, stand like statues, wait for the signal. The order is given; a loud screeching blast rends the desert air. The people let out a mighty shout and de walls came tumblin' down!

That is the old, oft told, greatly cherished tale. What is its charm? Why does it refuse to die but lives on and still grips the imagination? There may be many answers, each may have truth. One reason is this, it is a parable of life. This story tells us what life is like; this is what the people of God experience on pilgrimage.

Every life has its promised land toward which it marches. This promised land is a dream that sustains us; it is a vision that lifts our eyes above the present experiences; it is a goal toward which we strive for fulfilment. The Jews visualized Canaan as a place where they would have freedom and political security; it was a land that flowed with milk and honey; it was a land that grew grapes so large that it took two men to carry one great cluster. It was a land that would be a benefactor to all peoples as they came to Israel to worship the one true and living God. But the Jews were only typical. Everyone moves toward his promised land.

This dream is seen clearest in the child. For the child there is always excitement ahead; adventure lies just over the next hill and the next day. In her autobiography, *Family Gathering,* Kathleen Norris, the novelist, gives a picture of an interesting childhood and youth. There were days of struggle but there was joy in struggle, there was peace in the struggle. She tells of anniversaries, of presents, and of holidays. She says, "Our grievous fault was abounding ambition. Nothing was ever in the ideal state it was presently going to be or ever anywhere near our goals. But we kept at them day and night . . . we drew endless designs of our dream-houses." Of course they drew "endless designs of their dream-houses," that is what youth always does, that is youth's promised land.

But, it is not only childhood and youth that moves toward the promised land, maturity and age does too. We believe in the promised land, we have to believe in it. We believe the time will come when we shall achieve success, when we shall enjoy the fruits of our labors, when we shall have family and friends, when we shall have status and statue; we shall have our own business or profession; there will be time to travel, to read, to fish and to hunt, to enjoy life as it was meant to be enjoyed!

It is this that gives joy and zest to life; it is this that wreaths the face with a grin and causes songs to burst forth from the heart; it is this that keeps a man from getting old in spirit before he is old in years, that keeps him from the doctor's office and from the hospital bed. For, it is true, still true, that "we are saved by hope."

And, there is nothing that can atone for a lack of this dream and purpose, this exhilaration that comes from a conscious effort toward some promised land. Any family, people, or nation that takes this dream from individuals or groups of individuals will have much to answer for as well as great present trouble on their hands. When asked how he painted such exquisite pictures, the Italian painter, Raphael, said, "First, I have a dream and a vision, then I paint around these."

When there are no dreams and visions there are no worthy paintings.

Of course, in poetry and in song the promised land has come to stand for heaven, the eternal life. The river Jordan is death; Canaan is the Father's house. We sing, "I don't want to cross Jordan alone," and "On Jordan's stormy banks I stand, and cast a wishful eye to Canaan's fair and happy land, where my possessions lie."

Every man has his promised land toward which he moves. This is the first basic lesson that is seen in this old story. The second great truth of the story is this, there is a Jericho blocking the entrance into every man's promised land. Jericho was the gate to the promised land from the south and west. It was astride the way that led to all the passes into the interior of Palestine. Jericho was a walled city; it dared the Hebrews to advance beyond it. The Jews had to deal with that obstacle. They could not go around it; they could not tunnel under it; they could not climb over it. They had to confront it; they had to deal with it directly. It was a case of "take it or leave it." Take Jericho or leave the goal of the promised land.

It is true of every worthy promised land toward which life moves. There is always a Jericho that has to be dealt with first; you take Jericho or you can forget your dream of the promised land. Sometimes Jericho faces us in the form of outright opposition. Think about the desire for world peace, it is an ancient dream, it is a present dream. If the present desire is not greater than ever before, the need for it is greater than ever before.

But, across the entrance to that promised land sits a stubborn Jericho. Give it whatever name you will. We may "change the name to protect the innocent" but the opposition is always there. The only way to get world peace is to deal with that obstinate Jericho. Or, your promised land may take the form of racial understanding, law and order, ecology, a stable home life, honesty and integrity in government, business, the professions, labor, entertainment, and sports, or a deep concern for creative and worthy renewal and evangelism within Christendom. Whatever the form your promised land may take, sitting astride its entrance is Jericho. That stubborn obstacle has to be dealt with.

Sometimes the opposition, Jericho, comes in the form of grief. It was this in the case of orchestra conductor, Sir Malcom Sargent. Listen to some of the Britisher's recordings. You may be led to feel that he never faced a Jericho of grief. Not so. Just as he was beginning his brilliant career he was stricken with TB. He was critically ill. For two years he fought the dread disease. It sapped his energy; it laid clammy hands on his body; it sought to break his spirit.

When he returned to his music and life stretched out before him again, his thirteen-year-old-daughter, Pamela, was stricken with polio. For six years she fought her gallant battle. Sir Malcom was constantly by her side or away seeking medical help or forcing himself to do a minimum of professional work that all of his profession not be lost.

One evening in Liverpool he was ready to direct a performance of Handel's Messiah. Just before the performance began he was handed a note. It informed him that he had better come at once; they were afraid that Pamela was dying. With that news in his mind and soul he raised his baton and directed the orchestra in the recitative, "Comfort ye, comfort ye my people, saith your God." Sir Malcom's biographer is quite sure that it was often from this experience, this "Jericho," that the musician came to a deeper and a more assured understanding of and communication with humanity.

Sometimes the difficulty represents itself in a form no more dramatic than continuous and boring routine. One of the difficult and disturbing words of the Bible is the one that cautions us not to be "weary in well doing." But, that is often the most wearisome "doing" of all. Simply to keep doing well with no seeming end in sight. One is not surprised that constancy against obstacles is necessary in youth; it might be expected for a time, but to learn that there is simply no relief, and, that there is not likely to be any relief anywhere or at anytime in life, that can be a shattering experience.

And, if the fact is placed in the more rarefied air of spiritual truth, what may we expect? Surely, if the Jericho's are present on the lower levels of life we cannot expect them to be absent on the higher. If we do so expect, "spects" will certainly be broken! God operates no "bargain basements."

There is a dramatic scene in the seventh chapter of Numbers. Moses is portioning out the units of transportation to the Israelites. Then this word, "But to the sons of Kohath he gave none because they were charged with the care of the holy things, which had to be carried on the shoulders." Run that out in any direction. The "holy things" always have to be carried on suffering shoulders and wounded hearts. Mechanical inventions and scientific discoveries have their place. The churches have no right to downgrade their place but rather have the responsibility of making wide and wise use of them; still, there are some things that have to be carried in a more personal and intimate way.

Which is to say that our old antagonist Jericho has to be confronted!

There is a third truth in the story that must not be overlooked. Every man moves toward a promised land; Jericho stands astride the main entrance to that promised land. Now this—there are resources available for conquering that Jericho. Man need not fight his Jericho battle alone. When Joshua was planning his campaign against Jericho, he had a vision of an armed soldier standing with sword in hand. Joshua faced the being with this question, "Are you for us or for our adversaries?" To which the being responded, saying that he was neither for Joshua nor for the adversaries; instead, he was captain of the armies of the Lord. As if to say, the Lord will not be commanded by you or your enemy. The Lord is concerned and involved in this mission. If you wish to enlist in his army and under his leadership well and good. At this, Joshua fell on his face and said, "What does my Lord bid his servant?" And the presence said, "Put off your shoes for the place you are standing is holy." Acknowledge God!

Man need not go forth to fight his Jericho's alone; he may have divine assistance. But to secure that assistance, man must recognize who God is and what his rights are. Man must get his marching orders from a divine command post. Let man remember that God is concerned and involved. That God is as interested, at least as interested, in conquering the Jerichos of life as man is.

This is not an isolated experience. Men have always had God's help in attacking their Jerichos, have always had that help when the men were ready to meet the conditions and receive the help. Joseph was sold into Egypt, but the Lord was with Joseph. The Hebrew children were thrown in the furnace of fire, but there was a fourth person in the flames and his countenance was like that of the son of God. The disciples were in the midst of the storm, but the Master came to them. The two on the road to Emmaus were joined by a third, and the disciples hearts were warmed as that third opened the Scriptures to them. Stephen was stoned to death, but he was aware of the Christ. Paul experienced the loss of all his friends but he said, "The Lord stood by me." John was exiled to Patmos, but he was in the spirit on the Lord's day and is not alone. We get help.

Let us "pause for station identification." This parable of life says that every life moves toward a promised land, that across the entrance into this promised land always stands a Jericho, but that in our private or corporate war against these Jerichos we do not stand or fight alone. We get help and that help comes from God. And, when we get this help the walls of our Jerichos come tumblin' down.

5

"MY FAVORITE THINGS"

It is probably unnecessary to give the sermon title's source. For it comes from the delightful musical, "The Sound Of Music." It sings of raindrops, roses, kittens, copper kettles, and packages.

We all have our favorite things. For example, my favorite food is homemade ice cream. My appetite for it helps me to understand the alcoholic; once I take the first mouthful it is difficult to stop. My favorite sport is baseball; the crack of the bat against "horsehide," the smell of hot dogs, and popcorn, the vehemence vented against the umpires, and the rollicking good fellowship, for in the bleachers you can find slap-happy democracy at its crazy best! My favorite vacation spot is the little village, high in the Blue Ridge Mountains of North Carolina, called Blowing Rock. My favorite poet is Robert Browning, long out of date by most people's measurements, but his voice still speaks to me as no other poet's voice does. My favorite hymn is Isaac Watts', "When I Survey the Wondrous Cross." My favorite book is, of course, the *Bible*. But, that has been called a "library of books," rather than a single volume. My favorite book in that "library" and favorite passage within that particular book? That is a difficult question. Different people would make different choices; the same person might make a different choice at different periods in his life, or under varying circumstances.

Some would choose the first verse in the Bible, Genesis 1:1, "In the beginning God . . ." For that takes care of a multitude of questions; in it you can hear Gabriel's trumpet note in *Green Pastures,* "Gangway, Gangway for de Lawd God Jehovah!"

Some would choose Deuteronomy 33:27, "The eternal God is thy refuge, and underneath are his everlasting arms." Many would turn to Psalm 23, for to them God is their shepherd. Isaiah 40 and 53 are very dear to many. While in the New Testament we may turn to the surpassingly beautiful Nativity story in Luke 2. The world turns its gaze, of course, upon the Sermon on the Mount, Matthew 5–7. John 3:16 would certainly be high on the list with the multitudes. It has been called, "The Little Bible." At certain times in life most would turn to John 14 with its "many mansions." Paul's beautiful poem found in 1 Corinthians 13 with its, "Though I speak with the tongues of angels" is a spot that calls us again and again

If a definite choice had to be made, and only one choice was allowed, there would be great soul searching, but I would probably choose the unforgettable passage in Romans 8:31–39. Read it in Phillips translation.

In writing of his personal reaction to translating Paul's letters, Phillips said that he approached his task with the determination that he would maintain an emotional detachment; yet, he found again and again that the material with which he was dealing was "strangely alive." He said it spoke to his condition in a most "uncanny" way. That, not just occasionally but almost continually, he was aware of the "living quality" of those "strangely assorted books." Well, I am sure that was especially true when he came to translate this particular passage that I chose as "my favorite thing." It is reported that when Moffatt came to translate this particular passage that he sat for three weeks with cold towels about his head trying to turn the "blazing Greek" into English!

Of course, the passage is heady *doctrine*. It is frighteningly theological. And, that means it has at least one strike against its getting the attention of modern man. He "couldn't care less" about a theological approach. Like the lady who said of the Christmas carols, "They are all so theological!"

Yet, a passage that has endured so long, been cherished by so many, and offers promises, so much of what is so desperately needed in our time, should be given a chance to be heard. As Dr. John Hutton, the great English preacher, was once beginning his sermon, he saw that one of his parishioners had already settled down for a comfortable snooze. Said Dr. Hutton, "I have always felt that if anyone can fall asleep while I am preaching he is entitled to do it; the blame is mine; I assume full responsibility. But a friend here this morning is taking an unfair advantage of me. He is going to sleep before I get started. No! No! That is wrong! We must start fair!" Well, I appeal for the same sort of sportsmanship. Let's all start even, "eagle eyed," as Browning put it. Give Paul, and give me, a preaching chance. Then, if at the end, you still feel that the passage is too "theological," so be it; the fault will be ours, yours, and mine, not Paul's.

To begin with, the passage takes a magnificent view of God. Now, it is fearfully easy to think unworthily of God. Of course, that is quite evident today with the extreme and rapid views of the "God is Dead" philosophers who sound like a peg-legged man on a tin roof having a fit. What we need to remember, however, is this: it has never been easy to think magnificently about God. Oh, it has not been so difficult to think of his holiness, of his judgement, even of his awesome power. But, it has been difficult to think of his love, his mercy, and his forgiveness. It is just here that this passage bears in upon us.

Paul begins by saying that God gave his Son to us, that Christ is God's gift. God "spared not his own Son." The words remind you of God's commendation of Abraham when he offered Isaac, "Seeing thou has not withheld thy son, thine only son from me." So, as Abraham did not spare his son, there and then, so God does not spare his Son here and now. And the words indicate an unusual closeness; it is not that God did not withhold "a" son, it is more intimate, personal, and costly. The language indicates "his own Son," or "his only Son."

Dr. John W. McGarvey saw the picture clearly when talking

to a broken hearted father whose son had died. The distraught
father cried, "Where was God when my son died?" Professor
McGarvey placed a hand on the father's shoulder and said, "My
dear friend, God was just where he was when his own Son
died." God "spared not his own son."

But, "delivered him up for us all." That is the second word
that Paul affirms in his magnificent view of God. God delivered
him up to suffering, to temptation, to indifference, to hostility,
to death, even to death on a cross. What a list of "offering ups"
to catalogue.

Biographers love to find in the childhood of their subjects
foregleams, pointers, of what the subjects become and achieve
in later life. Such as Washington and the cherry tree story,
Lincoln and the long walk to return the few pennies that he had
overcharged the customer. Repeatedly the "no room in the inn"
incident has been singled out as prophetic of what the Master
would face throughout his ministry. As the spiritual says it,
"They didn't know who you wuz." And, the hostility that
required the flight into Egypt. Somehow, Herod and his cohorts
knew the wisdom of stopping this "King of the Jews" early.
"Get him while he is a baby!" They seemed to say, "If he grows
up there will be trouble." He came incognito. He faced indifference, hostility, cruelty, and death.

And, Paul says that he did this "for us all." God "offered him
up" for the least and the last; no one was to be left out. In a
novel by Maurice Hewlett a man says to Couer de Leon:
"There was a Father, my lord King Richard, who slew his own
son, that the world might be better." Richard asks, "And was
the world much better?" "Beau sire," said the man, "not very
much. But that was not God's fault, for it had, and still has, the
chance of being better for it."

Yes, it does. God sees to that.

Notice the perceptive thing that Paul does next. He says that
with Christ God will freely give us all things. What I want you
to see here is this, God will give you Christ. There has been

much emphasis on the fact that Christ was given *for* man, that Christ was given *on man's behalf,* or *instead of man,* Paul does not quarrel with that. At other times and places he will emphasize it. But, here he says, "with Christ." No matter what benefits one may derive from a marriage the gift of the person is greatest. A wife may stand in place of a husband, stand there for many things, a good wife will; but, unless along with *for* and in the *place of* she gives *herself* then "sure bad is the bargain."

But the message does not end there. With Christ God will give you all things—"All this and heaven too." It is, of course, an argument from the greater to the lesser. If he gives you the greatest gift, he will not deny you the lesser gifts. It has been said that if the Father gives us the kingdom, he certainly will not deny us toll-fare along the way to the kingdom. This is the Father's gift and the gift is free, "He will freely give you all things."

There is another sharp truth here. Notice it is God who will be the judge of what we need. So often we want things that we do not need and need things that we do not want. It is encouraging to know that God will now decide what we need and see that it is given. He will give all that is needed for a joyous acceptance, for a rich relationship, for necessary growth and development, for creative ministry, and for eternal life in Christ.

It is said that a beggar once sought an audience with Alexander the Great. Legend has it that Alexander made it his boast that his subjects could approach him at any time and make any request. When this beggar appeared, without hesitation or apology, he asked for a farm for himself, a dowery for his daughter, and an education for his son. Alexander immediately granted all three requests. The monarch's ministers were amazed that the requests were granted. Alexander said, "I get weary of people who come to me in fear and timidity asking for small gifts. That beggar treated me like a king. He asked big!" Remember on one occasion Paul wrote about God who, ". . . is able to do exceeding abundantly above all that we ask or even think."

God is honored when his children "ask big." For, he is a God who loves to "give big!"

This favorite passage not only gives a magnificent view of the love of God, it also gives a sublime view of the work of Christ. "Who will accuse us, blame us," asks the apostle, "it is God who justifies." Now, I am glad that Paul raises that question. As teachers are prone to say, "that is a good question." The matter of guilt is a problem to modern man no less than to ancient man. Every psychiatrist and physician and counselor knows that this is a serious battlefield. Nervous breakdowns, ulcers, heart failure, fatigue, low production, antagonism—these are only a few of the areas that received their undue reward from guilt and condemnation. Dr. Paul Tournier, the brilliant, understanding, and sympathetic Swiss psychiatrist has said that all men feel guilty, that guilt is a symptom and a disease of the twentieth century.

Perceptive artists know the poignancy of this need no less than physicians. What would the novelists do if they were not able to dissect the soul's of the guilt laden! That is pertinent all the way from Hawthorne's *Scarlet Letter* to *The Fall* by Camus. The central character in Camus' novel is a Paris lawyer. He is secure in his status and self-esteem. Then, one night, while walking home, he crosses a bridge over the Seine. Then it happens. He tells about it. He says that he had gone about fifty yards when he heard what seemed to be a body striking the water. Then he heard a cry, it was repeated several times; it seemed to be going down stream. Then he heard the cry no more. He said that he wanted to run, yet he did not; he stood still. Then he turned in the rain and slowly went away. The next day he told no one; he did not read the papers. But afterwards the memory of the incident haunted him. Years later, still carrying the deep sense of guilt, he cried: "O young woman, throw yourself in the water again so that I may a second time have the chance to save both of us. It's too late now, it will always be too late."

Man, all men, stand accused and the better the man, the more sensitive he is to his failures. The law condemns, conscience condemns, evil condemns, goodness condemns. The evil we do condemns us; the good we do not do condemns us; the social evil of which we are an inevitable part condemns us; our ignorance condemns us. We are constantly being reminded. We, along with Shakespeare's, Iago, are constantly meeting these Cassio's whose daily beauty makes us ugly. Years ago there was a delightful song from a movie that announced, "You could be better than you are," and went on to talk about swinging on stars and carrying moonbeams home in jars. Whether others say it or not, we know that we could be better than we are.

It is to that gnawing and yapping condition of guilt that the apostle speaks. He says that no one (or no thing) has any right to accuse us for God, "the only just Judge" has made us free from sin. He says that there is only one person in existence who has a *right* to condemn. That is Christ. Christ is the evaluator of all men; he is thoroughly qualified to judge, but instead of receiving condemnation from Christ what do we find?

Look to arguments: Christ died for man; if he was willing, and actually did die for man, will he be eager to condemn? Christ arose; that proves that God was pleased with and approved of what Christ had done and the way he had done it. Christ is at the right hand of the throne of God. That is additional proof that the Saviour did his task well; the "right hand" position was always saved for special favorites. Christ is, according to Paul, at the right hand of God looking after our interests. For, he is there to make intercession for us, to represent, and to answer all accusations. Elizabeth Barrett was a Christian poet when she wrote of Peter's denial of Christ and the look of the Master that sent the apostle out to weep:

> Go, and manifest
> A late contrition, but no bootless fear!
> For when thy final need is dearest,
> Thou shalt not be denied, as I am here;

My voice to God and angels shall attest,
Because I know this man, let him be clear.

Professor William Barclay has called attention to a pregnant idea at this point in Paul's case. Barclay says that one of the earliest creeds of Christendom, the creed that goes far toward embodying the essence of all Christian creeds, says: "He was crucified dead and buried; the third day he arose again from the dead; and sitteth at the right hand of God; from which he shall come to judge the quick and the dead." That is the early creed. Now, see what Paul does. Three items of the creed Paul latches on to: crucified, dead, and buried, and is at the right hand of God.

But, the *fourth* point is different. In the creed, the fourth point says that he will come to judge the quick and the dead. But, in the place of that, Paul says that *Christ is at the right hand of God to intercede for us.* It is as if Paul is saying: "You think Christ is a judge; well he may be; he has that right; he has the qualifications, but instead of being at God's right hand to judge us, he is there to intercede for us. He is not there as judge or prosecutor; he is there as an advocate; he is there to help; he is not there to state the case against us; he is there to state the case for us. He is there as friend and Savior. Does anyone wonder that this passage of Scripture is one of "my favorite things!"

It gives a magnificent view of the love of God; it gives a sublime view of the work of Christ. Take another step, see that here is a triumphant view of the Christians present and future condition. In this section Paul begins by talking about "separation." "Who," he asks, "shall be able to separate us from the love of Christ?" He then gives a long list of the things that often cause separation: trouble, pain, persecution, lack of clothes, lack of food, danger to life and limb, threat of force of arms, daily killings, and being led like sheep to the slaughter.

What a list! Yet, the apostles say that he is and that through all of those things "we win an overwhelming victory!" That is; that we are "more than conquerors." Then he gives another list of things that Christians were facing in that day, and, some of which, men face in every age. In spite of these, he says "I have become absolutely convinced that they cannot separate us from Christ." Look: death, life, angels (messengers), principalities (monarchs of earth), powers, things present (what happens today), things to come (what may happen tomorrow), heights & Depths (power from on high or from below), any creature (anything else in God's whole world).

The love of Christ, says Paul, is greater than any or all of these. They simply cannot separate us from the love of Christ. Does that mean our love for Christ, or Christ's love for us? Probably both are included, but especially the latter.

Occasionally we find a human love that surmounts many of these separations, and when we do, the spirit of man bows in gratitude before it as his spirit bows before few things. For example, there is a lovely and tender little book written by James Davidson Ross called *Margaret*. It is the true story of a young girl, fifteen years of age, who died of cancer. The book was written by her brother-in-law. He writes so beautifully, so tenderly, and so understandingly that you lay the book down with tears in your eyes, a sob in your heart, and yet with a shout of victory rising from your soul. The girl dictates her last will and testament; she dictates from the depths of pain. On the surface her bequests seem so small and trivial: a small piece of rope to her father, a locket to her sister, a prayer book to her brother, several toys to her nieces.

Then, along with these material items comes a more precious bequest: "To everyone who has been so wonderful to me these past months, I leave my love, my trust and my faith in Christ." For her brother-in-law she gives her most priceless bequest. She wrote: "To Jim: My savings certificates and myself: Lo, I am with you always, even unto the end of the world."

It is a beautiful message. Nothing short of the triumphant

realization of what Paul writes about in this passage of Scripture makes *Margaret's* experience possible.

The World Council of Churches closed its second session with the following words: "We do not know what is coming, but we do know Who is coming. It is He who meets us every day and who will meet us at the end, Jesus Christ our Lord. Therefore, we say to you, Rejoice in hope!"

6

"MAKE NO MORE GIANTS, GOD"

We all like Superman. That is true whether he is presented in a comic strip, a television program, a Nietzsche philosophic ideal, or in flesh and blood. It is the superman, or woman, the genius, the wonder-worker, the five talented individual who gets our attention—the most beautiful woman in America, the richest man in the country, the greatest athlete in the conference, the most experienced astronaut in the world, the best actress of the year, the author of the best seller of the season.

This yen for the wonder-worker is not new. It was as true in the first century as it is in the twentieth. The crowds milled about the Master. There was no time for him to eat or sleep; he could not withdraw from them even for a few days or hours of rest and relaxation. He said that they came because of his miracles. No matter how diligently he warned, no matter how carefully he cautioned, the news of his wonder working powers spread and the crowds came.

This is a disturbing truth. For one thing we are not wonder-workers. The majority of us are not, anyway. We do not have the most beautiful faces, the strongest bodies, or the most brilliant minds. We do not live in the best houses, drive the most expensive cars nor do we always reside in the most exclusive parts of the city. We are not among the "ten best dressed women," nor are we listed among the five most eligible bachelors. The truth of the matter is this: *we are ordinary human beings.*

We have normally functioning bodies; we have reasonably clear minds. We have homes and families, businesses, professions, or jobs. We are normally reliable; we can be depended

upon to do the decent thing, sometimes even the heroic thing in
a clinch. We love our families; we are decently patriotic; we give
acceptable allegiance to Christ and his church. We are normal,
ordinary, acceptable, run-of-the-mill people. Like Mark An-
thony, we are just "plain, blunt men . . . speaking right on
telling the people what they do already know." Occasionally,
but only occasionally, "showing wounds and asking that they
speak for us."

And, yet, we would like to be on the "side of the angels." We
earnestly desire a share in the triumph of the kingdom. We want
to be used. We crave the right to answer, "present," when the
roll of the faithful is called. What about it? Is there hope for
persons like ourselves? This sermon would speak to that situation and to those questions. It seeks to do so by relying upon a
biblical character who fits our mold. This man was no wonder-
worker; he performed no miracles. He just lived his life, served
his God, and died for faithfulness. This man was John the
Baptist. And, the scriptures say of him, "John did no miracle;
but all things that John spake of this man were true. And many
believed on him there." Consider:

John performed no miracle, but he revealed a strong character. Often you are asked to give a character reference. Usually,
the request is not for what the person has done, where he has
studied, or where he has been. It is rather, a request for a
character evaluation; what kind of person is this individual? If
you were asked to write a character reference for this man, John
the Baptist, what would you write? How would you react to the
following?

Dear Sir:
This word is written in response to your letter requesting a character reference for one John the Baptist.

This man is honest and truthful. He will swear to his own hurt and
never change. He is loyal to the highest and the best that he knows,
cost what it may. He is wise, having the strange ability to recognize

true greatness when it appears in a person no matter how carefully it may be concealed. He is courageous in person and in speech. He fears not the face of man; he calls his shots as he sees them, cost what it may.

He has perseverance, once he puts his hand to the task you can count on him to see it through to completion, no matter how hard the going gets, no matter what the lack of appreciation may be, no matter how he may be criticized or persecuted.

He is humble. He never tries to usurp the place of a superior. He recognizes his place and stays in it. He can and he will place others above himself. He can fade into the background and give another preeminence.

I should warn you that he is not the most diplomatic person in the world. He has a way of speaking the truth, the whole truth and nothing but the truth, as he sees it. He is not especially concerned about who gets hurt by this; he seems to feel that the truth is the truth and that he does not have to trim it, or be diplomatic in its presentation, or spend time in making it palatable to sensitive and tender taste buds.

In all honesty, this has been known to get him in trouble with the boys, and the girls, of power and influence who feel that they should be handled with kid gloves and nothing derogatory about them, their personal lives and administration released to the press.

But, if you want an honest, truthful, loyal, hardworking, wise, courageous, human, and humble man, you can do no better than to get Dr. John Baptist. He works no miracles but you can count on what he tells you about Jesus, and you will find that many people will believe on Jesus because of the testimony of Dr. John.

Yours truly,

Would you be willing to sign your name to such a character reference? If you are familiar with the biblical record you would have no hesitation in signing it, for, basically, the scriptures support the statement in its totality. A person does not have to be a wonder-worker, a performer of miracles, in order to have a great character. Character does not require great gifts, it can put down roots and grow in commonplace environment. It is possible for an ordinary, normal, run-of-the-mill man to be an honest, true, loyal, humble, and human man. And, do you know of anything that is more needed in the home, in school, in the field, forest, office, laboratory, assembly line and the space ship, than this sort of character?

"Speak truth; right wrong; follow the King; else wherefore born?"

Look again, John performed no miracle; yet, God had a special task for him to perform. That task pointed out in several directions. For one thing it pointed in the direction of the past and the future, the new and the old. John closed the door on the old and opened the door on the future. He was the last to sound the note of the old prophets of Israel, and he was the first to announce the arrival of the Messiah. With one hand he held on to the best of the past, with the other he reached forth to the good and great in the future. John was a sort of bridge over which the old and the new passed back and forth; in him the old saluted the new and the new made obeisance to the past.

That points up a great need. The generation gap that we hear so much about is not new; it has always been present. Yet, it is more intense today. The young discount age and tradition; the mature and aged devalue the emphasis and contribution of the young. This fact is seen in home, school, entertainment, business, professions, and government. Homes, schools, businesses, and churches cannot be operated and conducted as they were fifty years ago.

Yet, unless something of the character and the integrity of what was known in these institutions and areas at their best fifty years ago is continued in today's expression, the world will suffer seriously. And, how much more true it is of the ringing bugle notes of the prophets of Israel, that "glorious company of the blessed apostles, and, above all, the Lord Christ himself. Aye, we need John!"

Another direction of the task that John performed was in preparing for someone who was greater than he. John said that one was coming who was greater than he; John said that that One had to increase while he, John, had to decrease. This is a needed work; and, it is a difficult work to accept and to perform. The old word has it that we all want to play Hamlet; we want to occupy the center of the stage. Yet, the work of parents, teachers, prophets, priests, and poets finds its deep significance at this point, preparing for those who are greater than we are. Fortunate is the individual who is busy carrying out that task.

Notice, too, that John did the work that was given him in his own way. From the point of view of where John lived, what he wore, what he ate, what he said, and how he said it, John was unique. He did not lockstep it with his contemporaries; he listened to his own drummer and kept step with the music that he and he alone heard. Granted, that can be carried to the extreme; a man may be out of step with his fellows simply because he can't keep step with them, or he may be out of step because of just plain cussedness. But, few will question that life needs individuals like John, individuals who are not carbon copies but genuine originals, persons who do the work allotted to them, do it in their own way, to the very best of their ability and do not gauge their success or their failure by what others do or do not do. John was that kind of man. You can be that sort of person for it takes neither genius nor the power of the wonder-worker.

Take another look, John performed no miracle, but he was an unforgettable personality, for God and good. Who is your "most unforgettable character?" Each of us know a few characters who might be contenders for that place of distinction. Check it, is there one of those who could be called a miracle worker? Not on my list. Not a one! Let me nominate two. First, "Miss Cora." She was unmarried, worked as a clerk in a department store, and taught a group of ten-year-old boys in our Sunday School. "Miss Cora" did not have a car. She walked to the church, and she walked to the homes of the boys in her class.

Occasionally if the weather was bad we would ask someone to take her to the more distant homes. I have had these persons who took this little woman for her visits to the homes of "my boys," as she called them, come back with excited reports. "You should have been along," they would say. "You won't believe it! It is incredible! Do you remember that boy, Blank, that used to be such a terror. Well, we finally found the little house. We knocked on the door. The door was eased open about two inches, and then, "I am 'Miss Cora', Blank's Sunday School teacher, and I have come for a little visit." The door flew open; from an excited face, "Oh, 'Miss Cora,' I am glad you have come; I have been wanting to see you and to thank you for what you are doing for 'Blank,' you have no idea what you have meant to him. He is not the boy he was before he entered your class. I have no more trouble with him. I do thank you!" No genius here, no five talented person, just an ordinary human being with an extraordinary love for boys.

Another nomination. For many years I went on a Sunday afternoon to a cemetery where I met a small group of men gathered around a grave. The time was deep winter; I have met them when the snow was deep and was still falling. Some of these men had travelled far, using whatever means of transportation was available. They represented labor, business, the professions. They were middle-aged men now, some were gray-haired, some were bald. There about the grave I led the group in a brief memorial service. Frequently, if the weather was agreeable, I would ask one of the men to speak a brief word. The note sounded was always the same, though expressed in different terms.

Their words might be summed up in this way: "I was wild, reckless, heading straight for hell, when she got hold of me. She never gave up until she got my feet firmly planted upon the 'straight and narrow path'; today and everyday I thank my God for her and her love." A genius? A miracle worker? No, just a normal, ordinary woman who taught a young men's Sunday School class and whose name never made the headlines until the day when she was killed in an accident. But, she was an unforgettable character to those young men now grown to mature manhood.

Take another step, John performed no miracle, but he bore an effective witness for Jesus Christ. He did this not only during his life, he did it after his death. John was dead, beheaded through the vindictiveness of an evil woman; Jesus went back into the territory where John's ministry had been performed. The people still remembered John and his influence was still making itself felt. People were still believing on Christ because of the words and the life of John. If one is to be an effective witness for Christ, both words and life are essential, not life alone, not words without the life. But, a deeply devoted and faithful life plus courageous words, is always an effective witness. It is not necessary that a person be a genius; it is only necessary that a person be true, warm-hearted, and vocal.

Rummage in your memory, inquire of your minister, ask the evangelist who are the most effective witnesses for Christ. The answer will probably reveal a group of ordinary human beings who have shown forth an extraordinary devotion. In my youth I knew such an individual. For twenty-five years he had been superintendent of the little rural Sunday School. He could neither read nor write, could only make his "mark" on a check. He was a fine farmer; he was known over the county, respected by all, but seriously limited in many ways. Yet, he was not limited in his witness for Jesus Christ. I have seen his radiance, his quiet love and joy, his personal experience with the Lord move young and old to a new or a deeper commitment of life.

Once a secretary brought to me a package of cards. On each card was the name of an individual. In studying the names I recognized that here were some of the most dynamic, warm, participating Christians I knew. In their homes, places of business, and in their church life they were on "the first team." It was difficult to imagine what would be the effect upon the life of a great church were those fifty-eight individuals removed from its life. Yet, five years before, to the day, the fifty-eight individuals had become a part of the life of that church. At the close of the regular hour of worship each had presented himself, herself, for membership. What was the explanation for fifty-eight individuals presenting themselves for membership in a church at a "regular" service? Simply this, during the past week a group of normal, average, run-of-the-mill people had gone out into the community to bear their witness. The witness had been effective. Five years later I was looking at the names and expressing deep gratitude for the effective witnessing power of ordinary human beings.

There is a further word that needs to be said about this man John. He never performed a miracle, but he received great praise from the Lord of life. Christ said that of all the men in the past who were born of women (that took in most of earth's sons!) there had never been a greater than John the Baptist. Call the roll: Abraham, Isaac, Jacob, Joseph, Isaiah, Jeremiah, Amos, Hosea, go on with your name calling, according to the Scriptures, none was greater than John. Yet, he never performed a miracle.

Men need approval. If they are to remain mentally balanced and perform effectively in this world men have to have approval. The desire for it explains the strange conduct of many people. Well, for the followers of Christ, when at their best, there is no reward more earnestly desired than the "well done" that the Master bestows. Remember, and forget it not, in order to receive this approval one does not have to be a wonder-worker. Let a person, any person, any normal, ordinary, run-of-the-mill person, so commit his life to Christ that he is willing to die for his faith, and, does live for it, and he will receive the Master's "well done." That statement is based on good and adequate authority.

7

"WHAT ARE YOUR BOUNDARIES?"

John Steinbeck wrote a poignant story that he called, *The Leader of the People*. It is the saga of an old man who in his prime of life led a wagon train across the desert all the way to the Western coast.

It was a thrilling experience. There was adventure, excitement, hardship, danger, and death. The Indians were unfriendly; every mile of the way was disputed ground. Once the redskins drove off all the horses in the darkness of night. Once the people got so hungry that they began to butcher their own work animals, and, so, would have eaten themselves into starvation.

The leader had to be on guard at all times. He had to think for the people; feel for the people; plan for the people; he had to act for the people. But the old man had been equal to the task. He never faltered. He led the wagon train safely, led it all the way across the plains right up to the ocean's edge, would have led it further had there been anywhere else to go, but there wasn't and so there he stopped, right by the side of the ocean.

That day when the wagon train reached the ocean's edge the old man ceased to live and began a mere existence. For when that job of leading was done the old man's life was over. It had been a big job; he had done it well; but, the job hadn't lasted long enough. Now, there was nothing left for him to do but to think and talk about the past.

And talk about it he did! Talked about it to everyone who would listen, told his stories of crossing the wilderness with boring repetition. They were always the same stories. The old man's tone would drop into its narrative groove and the stories would drone on and on, speeding up for the attack, growing sadder over the wounds, striking a dirge at the burials on the great plains.

On and on he would talk with tiring monotony.

Carl, his son-in-law, was impatient with the old man. "How many times do we have to listen to the story of the iron plates, to the Indians driving off horses, to the people eating their own stock? That time is done; why can't he forget it? . . . He came across the plains. All right! Now it's finished! Nobody wants to hear about it over and over again."

Really, the old man did not want to be boring. But the crossing was the main thing in his life. It was significant not because of the buffaloes and the Indians, the adventures and the sacrifices. It was significant because the great mass of the people were made into one big crawling beast. And he was that beast's head. Each man wanted something for himself but the big beast, the beast that was all the people, wanted only westering. When they saw the mountains they cried. They had brought life out to the West and had set it down as ants carry eggs. Now, they were at the ocean's edge; there was nowhere else to go. The old man simply had to talk about the experience.

There was only one person who never grew tired of the old man's stories, that was Jody, his grandson. Jody was always eager to listen; Jody never became impatient. The events seemed to speak to a deep need in the boy. One day as the old man was coming to the end of his narrative, Jody looked up, smiled, and said, "Maybe I could lead the people someday?" His grandfather said, with sadness, in his voice, "There's no place to go, Jody. There's the ocean to stop you." And, the boy responded, shyly, "In boats I might, sir."

The old man only lived in the past. It was the past, and only the past, that gave his life meaning. It is a danger that is ever with us. It is easy to romanticize and glorify the past, to weave a spell of sanctity about it, to endow it with tradition, to link it with the fathers, to see it as a sacred heritage that has been bequeathed to us from those we "loved long since and lost awhile."

The power of such a memory and such a tradition are formidable indeed. They not only charm and comfort those who were an actual part of the events, but they are passed on to the descendants of the original participants. In this way ideas, habits, customs, institutions, and laws become so entrenched that they continue long after their usefulness has ceased, and, long after the spirit that brought them into being originally would give them sanction.

Just let a man, or a group of men, stand upon some soapbox, or its equivalent, and shout loud enough, long enough, and often enough, the slogan, "God forbid that I should give the inheritance of my father's unto thee!" and a sizable number of persons are ready to join in a crusade of preservation or restoration of any antiquity that has outlived its usefulness, determined to force the future's portals with time's rusty key. Jesus said to those who were doing just that, "You make void the word of God by your traditions."

Any careful consideration of church history is revealing at this point. Christianity itself broke the old wine skins of Judaism and became a separate movement because Judaism could not, would not, welcome the new wine of Christ and his message. Much of the history of the different denominations goes to this truth for light. There was a looking back with a refusal to welcome the new day, its needs and opportunities. Consider the life and work of Luther, Calvin, Knox, Wesley, and William Booth.

The past is valuable. It is not the entire war. It is an important battle in that war, a battle that is necessary to the successful prosecution of future battles. However, it is seldom that past battle plans, even when those plans were successful, can be duplicated in present battles. New occasions call for new duties. But, there is another view that is as dangerous as the backward view of the old man.

Carl, the son-in-law was impatient. He had no appreciation

for, no evaluation of, no ability to make use of the past. His
attitude: "How many times do I have to listen to those old
stories . . . That time's done, why can't he forget it . . .
Nobody wants to hear about it." To him today was entirely
independent of yesterday. He did not realize that without yesterday, today, as we know it, would be utterly unintelligible, even
nonexistent. For, the present always takes its stance upon the
tired shoulders of the past. It has been said of our relation to
those great minds who have gone before, "We are like dwarfs
seated on the shoulders of giants. We see more things than the
ancients and things more distant, but it is due neither to the
sharpness of our sight nor the greatness of our statue; it is
simply because they have lent us their own."

Moses is unable to lead the people into the Promised Land;
that is the job of a new man, a Joshua. The new task calls for
new plans, new initiative, new insights. But, all of this is directly
related to the work and the leadership of Moses. It was this
assurance that gave courage to Joshua. God said to him, "As I
was with Moses I will be with thee." There is the basic continuity.

To be mindful of the past should not mean an imprisoning of
the present within that past. It should mean that we continue the
tasks of today with certain capital bequeathed to us by yesterday. That we have an obligation to those who have gone before
not to rest upon their achievements and try to substitute their
victories for our own should go without saying. The words of
Pope are appropriate, "Boast not the achievements of thy ances-
tor's proud youth; they are their possessions none of yours." By
all means! Without today and its own contribution the salvation
of the past is incomplete.

Still, the present must have a good working agreement with
the past. Worthy education may never safely ignore this truth.
The truly educated man has his mind and character shaped by
the times, events, and persons that have gone before. An unedu-
cated person is one who is imprisoned within the present. He

does not look before and after for he does not know what was before, and he can have no worthy vision of what may be after. He is surrounded by no "cloud of witnesses," out of the past. He who denys the right of franchise to the past will be unable to pass a worthy franchise to those who are to come after him.

On Sunday, January 19, 1969, *The Los Angeles Times* had an editorial on President Lyndon B. Johnson. The next day, president elect, Richard M. Nixon, was to be inaugurated as America's thirty-seventh, president. The *Times* editorial was headed: "Johnson Era: A Summing Up." Here is a central paragraph from the editorial:

The Times' own judgment is that Mr. Johnson will leave a large and indelible mark on the history of this country because of the sheer magnitude of what he set out to do. He has not ended poverty nor guaranteed every citizen a life of dignity and purpose, but *he has made it impossible for future presidents to remove the commitment to such goals from the American agenda.*

There is history passing on capital in the form of obligation and responsibility to the present and the future.

But the past does more than assess responsibilities; it extends help. This is almost a mystical contribution. Suggestions, leads, intimations of just what it is and how it works have often been given, never with entire satisfaction. But, the reality few thoughtful men will question.

Tradition has its dangers, but to dispense with it is a greater danger. Fortunately we do not have to choose between the old man and Carl. If we were forced to do so, the decision would be a difficult one to make. They need each other; we need both.

Jody, the young grandson offers hope. He loved and appreciated the past. It spoke to something deep within his spirit. And yet, what the past said to him had to do with what was ahead of him, not just behind him. The past made Jody want to "lead the people." The past infused him with courage and hope to believe that he could "lead the people." He was not wedded to past methods, to horses, and wagon trains. He thought in new terms. When his grandfather reminded him that there was nowhere to go, that the ocean had stopped them, Jody said, "In boats I might, sir." Yes, in ships Jody might be successful; he might become another leader of the people. Look at a few of the "ships" that the "Jodies" of today will need if they are to become effective and safe leaders of the people.

In and through sonship time, all time, is redeemed and becomes one. And, that one time is a friend. The past becomes a vast depository that has on call the everlasting past, the eternal present, plus the unfilled tomorrows. To this fund the child of God makes his own deposits and he has his own withdrawal rights. God in Christ, who, we are assured, is "the same yesterday, today and forever," guarantees the account. Things that are present, things that have passed, things that are to come, things that are high, things that are low, things alive, things dead, things on earth, things in the air, absolutely nothing, will be able to confiscate those deposits. Sonship is an essential for effective leadership among the people. How does one become a son of God? Let the Scriptures speak:

We are children of God, and if children, then heirs, heirs of God and fellow heirs with Christ (RSV).

But to all who received him, who believed in his name, he gave power to become the sons of God, even to them that believe on his name.

Ye are all the children of God by faith in Christ Jesus.

Take a careful look at those pregnant passages and you will agree with Alexander Maclaren's analysis. First, inheritance depends upon sonship: children of God and if children heirs. Second, sonship depends upon a new beginning, a new birth: all those who received Christ were given the power to become sons, that is those who were born not of flesh and blood but by the spirit of God. Third, this birth depends upon Jesus Christ, for it is through faith in Christ Jesus that we become children of God. It is not by "screwing his will to the sticking point" that a man accomplishes this marvelous thing. It is rather, by the very energy and life of God within him that it is achieved.

Now, there is a "ship" that we must have if we are to lead. That assertion is not new. The apostle Paul affirmed it almost two thousand years ago when he said, "We are members one of another." But, we have been slow to believe the apostle.

On the bottom of the swimming pool at Monmouth, Illinois, the builders placed, at the center of the YMCA triangle the reference to a Bible verse. It was "John 17:21." A boy observed the reference but was unable to make out the wording. He dived and swam to the bottom. When the boy came up he said to the coach, "It says 'John 17:21,' but what is that?" His coach answered, "That they may all be one." The boy's response was more perceptive than he knew, "You sure have to go through a lot to find that out." Yes, son, we do. But, it is worth the effort.

On Christmas Eve of 1968 the Apollo astronauts flew over the surface of the moon. Earth was listening. The crew commented on the beauty of the earth as they saw it from that distance; they read the opening verses from the book of Genesis and invoked God's blessings on our sphere. The words and actions of the astronauts caused Archibald MacLeish to write the following, his words were released on Christmas Day.

"To see the earth as it truly is, small and blue and beautiful in the eternal silence where it floats, is to see ourselves as riders on the earth together, brothers on that bright loveliness in the eternal cold —brothers who know now that they are truly brothers."

As the boy in the swimming pool said, we "sure had to go through a lot to find that out." But, if we have really "found that out" it was worth all the effort. For we shall not be able to go much further unless we act on that discovery. Of the necessary qualities of leadership *membership* must be placed high upon the list. A man must be a real member of the group that he would lead. The group will forgive many inadequacies, excesses, weaknesses; the leader must identify with the group; he must have his *membership* intact. There is another necessary "ship."

A steward is one to whom something has been entrusted; it conveys the idea of responsibility to another. Stewardship, then, implies accountability. A steward is not a steward of what he owns; he is a steward of what another owns but has been entrusted to his stewardship. Sonship, membership, and stewardship, are all necessary, all available for the voyage to the future. It is difficult to see how the voyage can be successfully made under any leader's guidance without these. Certainly a man must have sonship. Until he is in proper relationship to God he cannot lead himself, to say nothing of leading anyone else; for, the man isn't going anywhere. Yet, there are multitudes who affirm that they are sons of God, and it is a confession that thoughtful men show humility in questioning. Yet, their ministry *seems* to end with having been adopted into the family of God. If they are aware that fatherhood and sonship imply brotherhood, the world is unable to observe it.

So, membership has to be included. The son must become aware that he is a brother as well as a son. The relationship is not just perpendicular; it is also horizontal. He lives in a family; he has to respect the members of the family. When Scott Fitzgerald died he left a suggestion for a short story. The notation given in his journal was of widely separated family that inherits a house in which they all had to live together. That is more than a suggestion for a short story; it is a parable of human existence. A man must own his membership. He probably could do that however, by having as his motto, "Live and let live." That is inadequate, certainly it is inadequate for the Christian.

Stewardship has to be added. A man must do more than "live and let live." He has to "live and help live." He has to be more than his brother's keeper; he has to be his brother's brother. He needs to be even more than that; he needs to be his brother's.

8

"LANTERN IN MY HAND"

"Thy word is a lamp unto my feet, and a light unto my path."

That line of poetry has been engraved upon the imagination of the believing world. It is not a word that can be remembered quite as much as it is a word that cannot be forgotten. Listen, "Thy word is a lamp unto my feet, and a light unto my path." Look carefully at those words.

"Thy word," that refers to the Bible. But, to the psalmist it meant more than written words. Again and again the poet's contemporaries, the prophets of God, affirmed, "The word of God came to me." They meant that they had experienced a direct encounter with God himself, not just words that an inspired man had written. Strickland Gillilan has it, "God kept on talking when his book had gone to press." He did and he does. Of course, the true, living, authentic word of God is Jesus Christ. John said, "In the beginning was the Word."

The word "lamp" in the text and the word "light" infer darkness. Were there no darkness there would be no need for a light. The text emphasizes the immediacy of the need. A lamp for the feet means that the need is personal; every man needs some assurance about where he is going to put his feet as he walks the roads of life. There is the suggestion, too, of a rough road; if the road were broad and straight and smooth there would be little need for a lamp even if darkness were upon the way.

Notice, again, that in addition to the parallelism of the verse there may well be the suggestion that God's word is a source of help in the light of day no less than in the dark of night. Listen, "a lamp unto my feet and a light unto my path." A lamp for the feet by night, a light, the sun, upon the path by day. The psalmist would suggest the need for God's word is as great in the day of success as in the night of failure. "Thy word is a lamp unto my feet and a light unto my path."

The truth of the text has been expressed in haunting lines by Joyce Kilmer in the poem "Love's Lantern" from *Trees and Other Poems,*

> Because the way was steep and long
>   And through a strange and lonely land,
> God placed upon my lips a song,
>   And put a lantern in my hand.

That says it. The way of life is steep and long; it winds through strange and lonely lands. Hence the need for lanterns and lights. That is not to sound a doleful bell and try to frighten pilgrims at the beginning of life's journey. It is, rather, to take a realistic look at life and see that reinforcements, lights, will be needed along the journey. The blind author, James Thurber, entitled his autobiography, *My Life and Hard Times.*

The explanation of the dark on the roads of life has challenged the best minds of the ages. Philosophers and poets have set forth their explanations, and when they have done their best they have acknowledged that they were, "unprofitable servants," and with the Queen of Sheba have cried, "The half was not told me." Three intimations may be helpful pointers to an understanding of "why" the darkness. First, we live on the earth; the earth is a part of the universe; the universe is regulated by a system of laws. These laws keep the universe in tune, "universe," "one-verse," but the laws are impartial. This means that if through ignorance, disobedience, imperfection, or rebellion we oppose these laws we get hurt, there is darkness. Second, we are bound in the "bundle of life"; we are not isolated units; we neither live nor die to ourselves. Even Robinson Crusoe had his man Friday. What others do casts light or darkness upon our paths. Third, God has granted freedom of will to man. Man does not always choose wisely, sometimes he does. Wise choices bring light; evil and foolish choices bring darkness. Most of the rough, steep, and dark conditions of life could be placed under one or more of these facts. However the experience may be catalogued, whatever explanation may be given to it, the experience itself cannot be ignored.

> Because the way was steep and long,
> And through a strange and lonely land.

Read biography and see the truth of those words. Few musicians have been as successful in wielding a large group of individual musicians into a single vibrating personality for interpreting great music as Arturo Toscanini. To have heard an orchestra under his direction, or even now to hear one of his magnificent recordings is to wonder if he ever knew darkness upon his way. Don't you question it! He was nearsighted; this made it exceedingly difficult for him to read the score when he was playing with the orchestra. So, he memorized every part he played. That he might be more sure of his own parts he memorized the parts of the other members of the orchestra. Just before an important performance the regular conductor was unable to perform. Toscanini, the nearsighted musician, who had memorized the entire score, was recommended as a substitute for the performance. When the concert was over the nearsighted youth was assured of a permanent place as conductor. He went from heights to heights until he was recognized as probably the greatest orchestra conductor in the world. The dark was to a large extent responsible.

Paul McElroy tells of an attractive girl stopping by a hospital bed to visit with a stone-deaf war victim. The youngster talked and the attractive girl wrote her answers on a pad of paper. As she was leaving, the deaf boy said, "Won't you come to see me again? It's awful not knowing what people around you are saying." The girl reached for her pad of paper, again she wrote. He read, "Oh, I don't know that it's so awful. I'm as deaf as you are. Why don't you learn to read lips as I have been reading yours?"

Darkness on the way. Van Wick Brooks gives it as his opinion that novelists thrive best on irritations. He says, "Hawthorne throve on the dust and wind of Salem. Flaubert, Stendhal, Sinclair Lewis, Dreiser are other cases in point; and do not Henry James' early novels show that this was also true for him? As long as he dealt with native Americans, who irritated him all the time, everything went well with James. England was too pleasant for him, and hence so much of his later fatuity. "Perhaps," he continues, "the less we satisfy our tastes, the more they serve to give us a scale and a measure." No new discovery this; the psalmist saw it, "God setteth the solitary in families: he bringeth out those that are bound with chains: but the rebellious dwell in a dry land."

There is no virtue in darkness for darkness sake. Let us rejoice for all light; let us be grateful for all humanitarians and all good social causes that make the lot of man easier. And, our concern at this point is greater than ever before. We are now ready to pass laws against all darkness and to legislate against all hardship. Well! But, forget it not, there is a razor's edge here between the hardship that cripples and the hardship that releases the spring of greatness. As we legislate against all darkness and hardship, let us be careful not to legislate against all greatness and excellence. Handicaps and opposition seem to have a vital part in producing greatness. Wright Morris once wrote, "If you are going to take the troubles away from a man —be careful what you take . . . You may take away the man instead of the troubles."

"Woe to them that are at ease in Zion." No tension, no muscles; no exercise, no strong body; no study, no mastership of mind; no lonely valley, no greatness of soul; the "fleas come with the dog." Greatness, it has been said, is like a Rembrandt portrait, it is an illuminated face shining out of a dark background.

> Because the way was steep and long
>   And through a strange and lonely land.
> God placed upon my lips a song,
>   And put a lantern in my hand.

Look at that "lantern." "Thy word," said the psalmist, "is a lamp unto my feet and a light unto my path." The Bible has been just that to the people of God. It is in and through the Bible that God speaks redemptively to his people. The Scriptures are his appointed means of communication. The Bible is not his only channel of communication. With Joseph Plunket we may see his blood on the rose, his eyes in the glory of the stars, his body amid the snows and his face in every flower; we may read his words in the rocks and find his footprints in all paths, and be reminded of his cross in every tree. Still, it is through and because of the Bible that we are able to see him and to hear him through these mediums. The Bible is the code book that makes it possible for man to interpret God in time and history. If you doubt it, inquire of peoples in lands where the Bible is unknown. They will tell you that they are unable to see and to hear God in nature.

In 1849, Dostoevski, the Russian writer, was banished to Siberia. There, for four years, he was herded with criminals in what was known as the "House of the Dead." Everything in his sensitive soul and mind cried out against that cruelty and inhumanity. But, Dostoevski carried with him into that "House of the Dead," a little book, the New Testament. He read it over and over. The burning flames of anger died down in his soul; he became a follower of Christ. Aften ten years of banishment he returned to his home a new person. From henceforth he was known as a philanthropist, a helper of the helpless and broken; a teacher of the Christian faith once delivered to the saints. George Brandes affirms that his death brought grief to the nation, and, even Nietzsche acknowledged the reality of his new life in Christ. The New Testament became a "lantern in his hand."

A few years ago the church of which I was minister gave me a sabbatical leave. I had been with the church for seven years; the year's leave was to be used for travel and study. The year was spent in two great universities, one on this side of the Atlantic, one on the other side. Never, "till death hangs his sickle on my garden gate," shall I be able to put into words what the year meant to me.

During that year I was a student of some of the best and clearest and most devoted teachers in the world. Yet looking back upon that experience from the distance of several years, I bear a witness. What meant most to me during that sabbatical year was not the universities and the teachers and the fellowship with students of kindred minds. What meant most to me, and what has continued to mean most to me since was the reading of God's word. I read it carefully, prayerfully, devotionally, lovingly, patiently. I read it for great blocks of time on through the night and into the early morning hours. I read it not for sermon building but for soul building; not to meet a deadline but to meet a life line. It became a lantern in my hand.

This word of God is adequate. Like the famous magic tent of which we read when we were young, a tent that could be folded and carried in a man's hand or unrolled so that it would cover armies, so this Bible of ours is a lamp for the feet of the individual and a light for the nations. Its light and truth are certain; there is no indefiniteness here. Christ said that heaven and earth would pass away, but that his word would not pass away. Both prophecies have come to pass. Under the picture of Peter Milne, in the church founded by him on Nguna in the Hebrides is a tribute that might well be ascribed to the word of God when it is appropriated; the inscription says:

> When he came there was no light,
> When he left there was no darkness.
>
> Because the way was steep and long
> And through a strange and lonely land,

> God placed upon my lips a song,
> And put a lantern in my hand.

We travel a long road, and that road is often dark. It winds through a strange and lonely land. To meet our needs God puts a lantern in our hands. And, he puts a song on our lips.

Just here we come upon a truth so strange that it passes understanding. It is this—the harder the road, the more hopeful the songs! Just when the road of life gets so dark and rough and steep and lonely that one would expect to find all voices muted, a great chorus of praise and thanksgiving breaks forth from the pilgrims. In all honesty it must be said that this is not always true. It is true for those who grasp firmly the lantern of God's truth. The greatest sufferers are often the greatest believers.

How can this truth be explained? How is it that God gives songs in the night? Is it that only those who have been in the darkroom of life can experience the development of the grace of Christ within the heart? That it is only in weakness that we are made strong, that it is only in illness that we accept the services of the Great Physician? Is Tagore's parable pertinent, that only the taut violin string is really free, and that it is only the free string that gives forth great music?

Could a domestic experience help? I once found it necessary to discipline my thirteen-year-old son. He was instructed to remain indoors for the day; he was not permitted to go outside during the entire day; he could not use the telephone, radio, or television. His friends could not call; he was to be isolated for the entire day. Granted, the punishment seemed rather severe and along in the afternoon I was ready to relent. At the dinner hour I reasoned it might be wise to relax the restrictions and let him use the telephone during the evening hours, for what can be harder on a teenager than to be denied the use of a telephone!

However, when I got home in the afternoon I did not find a dejected and grieving teenager, filled with self-pity. My son was in a mood of warm job and gladness; he even greeted me with enthusiasm and hearty goodwill. Explanation? I had overlooked the hidden resources of his mother. She had seen to it that my orders were strictly obeyed but beyond that her marvelous love and her great inventiveness had come to play. She and Perry had talked and talked. They had laughed and shared experiences. Bits of family history had been revealed to him that he had never known before. They had read and told stories. They had mapped out things they would do on vacation. It had been one of the richest and most significant days in the boy's life, and he was perfectly willing to have me level the same discipline on his head for another day—which I did not do!

May it not be close to a parable? Through illness, pain, grief, disappointment, we experience isolation. In and through that isolation there is time for thought, study, meditation, and a personal encounter with God. This close relationship, a relationship that we would never have taken time for under normal circumstances, so far outweighs any loss caused by the isolation from natural pursuits, that we find ourselves singing songs of praise and thanksgiving. "God placed upon my lips a song."

It has been said that the worst sentence ever passed upon Christians in the early days of persecution was to be sentenced to the mines of Numidia. This was a much worse sentence than being decapitated or thrown to the wild beasts in the arena or used as torches in Nero's gardens. The Christians were chained to the galleys and rowed to their doom. Arriving in Africa they were marched to the mouth of the mines. There they were seared on the brow with glowing irons, their chains were shortened so that they would never be able to stand erect again. Often one eye was knocked out. They were then given a lamp and a pick and sent into the mines to dig until they died, being watched over by merciless overseers. These Christians knew that they would never come out of the mines alive. Still, God placed songs upon their lips. Their radiant witness and their grateful prayers are recorded on the walls of the mines. It consists of one word, but that one word occurs again and again.

This is the word, "LIFE!" "LIFE!" "LIFE!" Enemies could shut them away from the world but no enemy could shut God in Christ away from them. In the darkness of the mines and the blindness of physical sight his word and presence became a "lamp unto their feet and a light unto their path."

> Because the way was steep and long,
>   And through a strange and lonely land,
> God placed upon my lips a song,
>   And put a lantern in my hand.

9

"THANK GOD A MAN CAN GROW"

"Though his beginnings be but poor and low,
    Thank God, a man can grow."

Those words of Florence Coats point to a deep seated desire on the part of man and beast. It is a desire to grow, a striving to achieve. The plant reaches toward the sun; the animal is a dynamo of energy; man "looks before and after and pines for what is not." Growth and fulfillment, a striving for maturity, this is a law of life. The poet asks, "Why stay we on the earth unless we grow." The greater the man, the higher the aim.

That low man seeks a little thing to do,
    Sees it and does it:
This high man, with a great thing to pursue,
    Dies ere he knows it.
That low man goes on a dadding one to one,
    His hundred's soon hit:
This high man, aiming at a million,
    Misses it an unit.

Now listen to one of earth's greatest of men express his highest desire for growth:

How changed are my ambitions!
Now I long to know Christ and the power shown by his resurrection:
    now I long to share his sufferings,
    even to die as he died,
    so that I may perhaps attain, as he did,
    the resurrection from the dead.

Yet, my brothers, I do not consider myself to have 'arrived,' spiritually, nor do I consider myself already perfect. But I keep going on, grasping ever more firmly that purpose for which Christ Jesus grasped me. My brothers, I do not consider myself to have fully grasped it even now. But I do concentrate on this: I leave the past behind and with hands outstretched to whatever lies ahead I go straight for the goal—my reward the honor of my high calling by God in Christ Jesus (Phillips).

How does a man grow in Christ? How does he gain stature and maturity; how does he achieve that for which God has called him to achieve? In the passage quoted above from Philippians 3, the apostle sets forth a four-point program. He says if a man is to grow in spiritual maturity, he must have a high aim, "That I may know him." It is possible that we shall not reach our aim; it is almost certain that we shall not go beyond our aim.

To know Christ is Paul's aim. No man can have a higher aim. By "knowing Christ" Paul does not mean *knowing about* Christ; he is not writing of an intellectual knowledge. That would be a worthy goal, but it would not be the highest goal. He does not mean *historical* and *factual* knowledge that can be gained simply by careful and diligent research. It is possible to have a great deal of knowledge *about* Christ, yet, have very little knowledge *of* Christ.

By knowing Christ, Paul means knowledge that is based upon personal experience; it is knowledge gained through intimate, personal union with Christ. For example, I knew about my wife for some years before we were married. I knew her name, the part of the country from which she came, something about her family, its size and numbers; and I knew the college she attended, her academic achievements and her student activities; I knew about her standing and her reputation in the field of her chosen vocation; I knew many of her friends. Then we loved and were married. Our love and relationship overflowed into children. In the biblical phrase, we two became one. Then I knew my wife; this knowledge was more than knowledge *about* her.

When Paul says that he desires to *know* Christ, it is the same word in Greek that is used in Hebrew when we read that Adam *knew* his wife Eve and she bare a son. It means that as a man and woman know each other in the marriage relationship, in the parent-child relationship, as a man knows his dearest friend, so Paul desires to know Christ; it is knowledge gained through a close, intimate, and personal relationship that he desires. It is the knowledge that is meant when the Bible says, "And this is life eternal that they might know thee, the only true and living God and Jesus Christ whom thou hast sent."

This knowledge involves a number of things. It involves experiencing the power of the resurrection of Christ. Again, this is more than a historical and intellectual knowledge about an event which took place in a little country called Palestine in the first century A.D. It includes this event; it is never entirely separate from it, but it is more than knowledge *about* this historical event. For the Christian, the resurrection is a living, dynamic, power and spirit that pulsates and empowers the life of the Christian.

For the Christian, the resurrection means at least four tremendous truths, each experienced in his own life; some Christians experience these truths more; some experience them less. First, it is a guarantee that sin is doomed; God and good win; Satan and evil lose. Second, it is a guarantee of the importance of this life that we live in the here and now. It was in the flesh that Christ came; it was as a man that the disciples knew him. Third, it guarantees the reality of everlasting life; and fourth, it guarantees that this everlasting life will be lived in fellowship with Jesus Christ.

In beautiful words, Joseph Fort Newton wrote about the death of his father in *River of Years*. The author was just a boy. Clinging to the hand of his mother, he looked for the first time into an open grave; it was a strange and terrifying experience for him. Then he writes, "The old country minister adjusted his glasses and read the words of Jesus, 'I am the resurrection and the life—Let not your hearts be troubled.' Never shall I forget the power of those words. It was as if a great, gentle Hand, stronger than the hand of man and more tender than the hand of any woman, had been put forth from the Unseen to caress and heal my spirit—from that day to this I have loved Jesus beyond the power of words to tell!" That is what Paul means by knowing the power of Christ's resurrection.

Knowledge of Christ involves entering into the fellowship of the sufferings of Christ. Attention has been called to Paul's order of knowledge and experience. You might think that Paul would place first his desire to know the sufferings of Christ and then his desire to know the resurrection of Christ. This is not the order he chooses. Paul's order is the correct order. It is only after one has experienced the power of the resurrection of Christ that he is capable of entering into the sufferings of Christ. In the sufferings of Christ, Paul means that even as Christ he would suffer for the sins of others; the sufferings of others would become a part of his sufferings; and he would suffer in the service of others.

The Christian who experiences the power of the resurrection of Christ enters into the walk, the work, the will, and the way of Christ. Mysticism, clear and simple!? Then we make the most of it!

The second point on Paul's program for spiritual growth is this: you must eliminate all unnecessary baggage. "This one thing I do," said Paul. Some years ago a traveling companion and I were flying out of Honolulu for Manila. As we were checking in at the airport, we discovered that we had excess baggage. That excess was costly. We had to pay seven dollars for every excess pound that we carried—that is, excess luggage; fortunately they did not weigh the passengers! The experience taught us to be careful about the number of items that we took with us on that trip.

Many people fail in life because they do not concentrate. They are like the song in Gilbert and Sullivan; "They do nothing in particular, but they do that exceedingly well." Gibbons said of the Emperor Gallienus that he was a ready orator, an elegant poet, a skillful gardener, an excellent cook, and a contemptible prince. Bismarck affirmed, "Hang me so long as the rope binds Germany to the Prussian throne." It was like Paul saying, "This one thing I do."

Here is the explanation of many failures. Individuals do not know how to say, "This one thing I do." The young wife does not say it, and her home goes to pieces. The doctor does not say it, and his practices fall off; the farmer does not say it, and grass, weeds, and erosion ruins his farm; the artist does not say it, and loses his skill. The student does not say it, and he fails his courses.

The difficulty is seldom at the point of ability; it is, rather, at the point of evaluation, selectivity, and concentration. The two-talented person who says, "This one thing I do," will outstrip the five-talented person who says, "These twenty-five things I do." This is one explanation of why the "average" students so often outdistance the "brilliant" student in the race of life. It is, too, the explanation why the minister of average natural ability so often does a mighty work for God. He has average ability, but he has extraordinary skill in the elimination of excess baggage; he allows nothing to interfere with his service in Christ's kingdom. Therefore, he grows.

> Though his beginning be but poor and low,
> Thank God a man can grow.

If a man has this burning desire, if it is first in his mind and heart, if he seeks to eliminate all that would hinder his pursuance of this goal and purpose, all life will contribute to his spiritual growth. For, make no mistake, it is not necessary that a man lead a monastic life in order to grow spiritually. The honest and constructive work that you do, the home that you love, the friends whom you appreciate, the books you read, the vacations you take, the food you eat, the clothes you wear, the songs that you sing, the words that you speak, will all contribute to your spiritual growth; provided you say in the presence of Christ, "This one thing I do."

Consider a third point in Paul's program for spiritual growth. We must choose our memories, "forgetting those things that are behind." A wise forgetfulness is essential to spiritual growth. Much is said and more is written about the importance of remembering. Magazine articles are written; books are published; courses are offered to help us remember. Many of us have seen one of these "memory experts" come into a civic club, or some other organization; and after being introduced to a hundred men, one hour later be able to call each of them by name. At such times, it is difficult for us not to break that commandment which says, "Thou shalt not covet!" For, we have experienced memory blockage and were unable to recall the name of our closest friend when we wanted to introduce him.

Still, the honest truth is this: most of us remember too much rather than too little. Many of us would pay more for a course that would teach us to forget than we would for one that would teach us to remember. The old Greek, Themistocles, prayed: "Teach me the art of forgetting; for I often remember what I would forget and forget what I would remember." The philosopher Kant once wrote himself a note when hurt by a man named Lampe. The note said: "Remember to forget Lampe." It does not take a professional expert in the field of mental health to tell us that it is often what we remember that is responsible for our undoing. For what we remember is far more than we can recall. It is often those whispering, gnawing, clawing, half-conscious memories of the past that destroy our peace of mind, make us ill, and make us do less than our best.

Now Paul comes and says, "No more of that for me; I shall forget those things that are behind." And we say to him, "Neat trick if you can do it! But to forget what you cannot help remembering is double talk; it is a contradiction in terms." And if Paul were speaking to us today, he might say: "In terms, yes; in experience, no; in logic, yes; in morals, no; in law, yes; in grace, no. For to literally remember and yet to spiritually forget is not only a possibility; it is the actual experience of multitudes; it was, at least, my own experience."

Of course, Paul is not advising that we forget everything. Indeed one of the great sins of Israel was that she so often forgot what God had done for her. Then she ceased to be grateful; and when this took place, she ceased to worship. The same is true of the individual. No memory, no gratitude; no gratitude, no worship; no worship, no service; then sin and weakness are inevitable.

Paul means that we are to forget past failures that would cause us to lose heart in the present and in the future. He means that we are to forget the failures that make us fearful; we are to forget the victories that would make us proud; we are to forget the sin, and the sins in the past, that would make us cowards in the present. It is fearfully easy to so remember our sin that we discredit God's promises to forgive. It surely is dishonorable to God to remember the sins that he forgets. Forget the past; face God and the future.

Finally, Paul says that if we are to grow spiritually, we must press on toward the goal; "I press on toward the mark of the prize of the high calling of God in Christ Jesus." If we have a worthy aim, if we eliminate excess baggage, if we choose our memories wisely, it remains for us to press toward the goal.

The figure of speech is significant. It is the picture of a runner racing hard toward the tape. His eyes strain ahead; his arms churn; his knees pump; his head stretches forward; his body is bent; his breath comes in short gasps; the blood rushes to every part of his body. This is the picture that Paul uses to express the way he feels about the Christian life. There is no suggestion of ease and indifference here.

We know the value of strenuous effort in other areas. John Morley explained Gladstone, the English statesman's freshness and enthusiasm by saying, "He kept himself upon the line of discovery." Ruskin wrote, "The law of nature is that a certain quantity of work is necessary to produce a certain quantity of good, of any kind whatever. If you want knowledge, you must toil for it; if food, you must toil for it; if pleasure, you must toil for it." "Nature," wrote Goethe, the German poet, "knows no pause, and attaches a curse to all inactivity." Emerson said of Napoleon: "Having decided what was to be done, he did that with might and main; he put out all his strength. He risked everything and spared nothing—neither ammunition, nor money, nor troops, nor generals, nor himself."

Strenuous effort in these areas we recognize and are quick to applaud. Yet, when it comes to spiritual growth, a grasping after that for which Christ grasped us, we somehow expect to drowse ourselves into the kingdom. We refuse to take the old spiritual seriously; "You can't get to heaven in a rocking chair; you'll rock right by them pearly gates." And, it is not only the "pearly gates" that we shall rock by, we shall rock past the possibilities for divine favor, growth, and human need in the present. John Bunyan wrote about the man with a stout countenance who after looking carefully, and weighing deliberately, the cost of the Christian life, went up to the one who had the pen and inkhorn and said: "Set down my name, Sir, for I have looked this whole thing in the face. Cost me what it may, I mean to have Christ likeness and will!"

> Though his beginnings be but poor and low,
> Thank God a man can grow.

Yes, he can!

10

"A HEART FIXED TO GIVE"

Out in the desert the note was found, written with a lead pencil on a piece of brown wrapping paper. The note was stuck in a rusty baking powder can that had been tied with a piece of wire to an old pump. The words scribbled on the paper said:

Under the white rock I buried a bottle of water out of the sun. cork end up. There's enough water in it to prime this pump, but not if you drink some first. Pour about one-fourth and let her soak to wet the leather. Then pour the rest medium fast and pump. You'll get water. The well never has run dry. Have faith. When you get watered up, fill the bottle and put it back like you found it for the next feller. Signed, Desert Pete
P.S. Don't go drinking up the water first. Prime the pump with it . . . I've given my last dime away a dozen times to prime the pump of my prayers and I've fed my last can of beans to a stranger while saying 'Amen.' It never fails to get me an answer. *You've got to git your heart fixed to give before you can be given to.*[1]

"You've got to get your heart fixed to give before you can be given to." Yes, you do! And we have it on better authority than "Desert Pete" although I never care to argue with experience. Yet, there is a better authority. Listen! "For whosoever will save his life shall lose it: and whosoever will lose his life for my sake shall find it." "It is more blessed to give than to receive," and "Give, and it shall be given unto you, good measure, pressed down . . . and running over," and "Give to him that asketh thee, and from him that would borrow of thee turn not thou away." Authoritative? Indeed! Those are the words of Jesus of Nazareth.

And if you wish to go into a more extended discussion of the truth consider the parables of Jesus. Think of the rich man and Lazarus; also, consider the parables of the judgement, and of the Good Samaritan. Then remember that the very basis of the Lord's coming to earth was centered in this truth. Paul said that Christ "emptied himself," held nothing back, gave until he could give no more. Then, he died, as if he had finished what he came to do, and having done that there was no need to linger longer. He came with his heart fixed to give.

The world approves of that. It believes that when the church is like its Master it will have its heart fixed to give. The man of the world has many criticisms of the churches; some of his criticisms are just, some are unjust. When he criticizes because the disciples of Christ do not have their hearts fixed to give, he draws an accurate bead.

This was once brought home to me in a disturbing way. I was minister of a downtown church. The sanctuary was a thing of quiet beauty, gothic in structure, deep wall-to-wall red carpet covered the floor, great organ, windows that told the ancient story of the Christian faith through exquisitely wrought art. The order of service conducted there was in keeping with the setting. On this particular morning the deacons had come forward, the offertory sentence had been spoken, and the offering of the people was being received while quiet and lovely music was speaking peace to the hearts of the worshipers. Then I *sensed* that something unusual had projected itself into that quiet and worshipful setting, *sensed* it; I had not *seen* it. Lifting my eyes and thought from the mood of prayer, I *saw* him.

He was standing by the communion table. His appearance was completely out of character with everything that I have described. He was dirty, ragged, disheveled; his eyes were far back in deep sockets whose rims were red; his gaze was focused on me. How he got down that long, beautifully carpeted aisle without being detected and assisted to an unconspicuous seat by one of our well trained and efficient ushers I never knew. But there he stood. Rising from my plush chair I bent over and said,

"Yes, what is it?" And this is what he said, "I'm hungry, what are you going to do about it?" Even at this distance, and it was years ago, the scene is too painful to tarry over.

Not to be misunderstood, it does need to be said that there are occasions when quiet worship is appropriate. Sanctuaries of beauty and symbolism have their place; Jesus loved the temple; it grieved him to think that it would be destroyed. He rose to the defense of an act of "extravagant love" on the part of a dark eyed maiden who anointed him. When reminded that the oint-ment might have been sold and given to the poor, he told the critics that there was a time for "extravagant" and "impractical" giving. And, that act of utterly "impractical giving" has proven to be one of the most "practical" of all acts. For, it might be said of that young woman, as was said of another extravagant act, "She has given more than all."

Still, that, "I am hungry; what are you going to do about it?" was an unnerving affirmation and question. At that moment, the beauty, the quiet, the separation, the isolation of the hour seemed irrelevant to the situation. Somewhere Ogden Nash has affirmed that religion does not compel one to love the pigeon. Maybe not, though apparently God does. Man, however, is not a pigeon; he is one who is made in God's image. And, when he says, "I'm hungry; what are you going to do about it?" it is time we get our hearts fixed to give.

Now, hark back to the New Testament lesson of the morning. The classic sermon outline on the parable of the Good Samari-tan runs this way: The robbers said, "What is yours is mine and I'll take it"—their hearts were fixed on *getting*. The priest and the Levite "passed by on the other side;" they said, "What is ours is ours and we'll keep it"—their hearts were fixed on *keeping*. The Samaritan "came where he was, had compassion, bound up his wounds, took care of him;" saying, thereby, "what is mine is yours and I'll share it"—his heart was fixed on *giving*. And, Jesus said, "Go, and do thou likewise."

There are those, who like the first characters in the story, have their hearts fixed on *getting*. It is seen in graft and greed and corruption, in organized crime, in hold-ups and kidnappings, in heartless competition and pressure groups, in lootings and burnings and violence. Their representative might be the New Zealand chief who declared that he was the rightful owner of a certain piece of property; when challenged to show his credentials, he said: "It is mine because I ate the former owner." Motto? "What is yours is mine and I'll take it."

Of course, the person who is reached by these words is comfortable as that type of "getter" is described. We do say, "Thank thee, Lord, that we are not as other men." And we may well be grateful, genuinely so, that we are not of that company. Still, the heart that is fixed on getting finds many outlets; it reveals its colors in less dramatic ways. One of Abraham Lincoln's neighbors in Springfield, Roland Diller, was attracted to the cries of children in the street. He went to the door and saw Lincoln striding by with two of his sons; the boys were wailing loudly. Diller called to Lincoln to know what was wrong with the boys. The answer: "Just what's the matter with the world," replied Lincoln, "I've got three walnuts, and each wants two." Kingdom or walnuts, the principle is the same.

The twentieth century is paying a fearful price for the "getting hearts." Ulcer lane, heart seizure executive suite, high blood pressure club, alienation country estate, frustration overnight jet, they all take their toll.

It might be well for us to read again Tolstoy's story that he called, "What Shall It Profit?" It tells of the "getting heart" of a man who went to a distant land where the head of the tribe promised to give him, for a thousand rubles, all the land he could walk around in a day. The man was instructed to put his money down at a certain spot and to start walking; all the land he enclosed before sundown would be his. The land hungry man started walking, faster and faster and faster, a little farther, a little farther, a little more rapidly; the sun was sinking; he must hurry; just a little more effort! He reached the point of his departure just as the sun was going down—but, his exertion had been too great; he fell dead at the point of his departure. He was buried; six feet of earth was all that he could claim. The parable is as relevant today as it was when Tolstoy first told it. It is dangerous to have the heart set on getting.

And there are those who have their hearts set on *keeping*. They do not "attack" the traveler, nor do they "eat the former owner." They cannot be accused of racing up the "status seeker" stairs. They "sit tight," they "have it made" and they mean to "keep what is theirs." They act as if all the lessons were learned and all the problems solved. Someone has said that they break no windows but neither do they light any lamps; they start no riots but they bring no yeast for peace; they tell no false-hoods but neither do they teach any truths; they do not tear down but neither do they build up. It is the mood, "What is mine is mine and I'll keep it." They have hearts that are fixed on keeping.

However disturbed we are over the rebellious and revolution-ary spirit that is such a real part of the late twentieth century, a part of that spirit is due to hearts that are "fixed to keep." One need not approve methods before he can endorese evaluations, and endorse with righteous indignation. Indeed, if we are to rightly interpret and nobly follow Jesus Christ we shall have to, as he, "look upon them with anger." And first, we shall have to turn that anger inward, for who of us is guiltless.

So much of the teaching of Jesus was aimed, not at hearts that were "fixed to get"; although he aimed some arrows in that direction, but at the point of those who were bent on leaving things as they were, letting "well enough alone," at those who said, "What is mine is mine and I'll keep it." This is the point of his story about the barren fig tree. He judged the tree not because it was bearing poison fruit, but because it was bearing no fruit. The rich man was condemned not because he was abusing and oppressing the beggar at his gate, but because the beggar was not being helped. The parable of the judgement is fierce in its condemnation, not because water was taken from the thirsty, bread from the hungry, not because of opposition to those who desired to visit the imprisoned, but simply because a positive, constructive program of help was not followed. Certainly the priest and the Levite did not abuse the man by the roadside, but neither did they give assistance. All these characters that Jesus so soundly condemned were like the character in Gilbert and Sullivan who did nothing in particular but he did that very well! Their hearts were fixed on doing nothing, fixed on keeping. The elderly lady was quite ill, and had been for a long time. She said to her minister, "I don't see why the Lord don't take me." Said the minister: "Well, sister, it must be because the Lord has a job for you to do." That idea was infuriating to the ill woman. She said, "Then I can tell you right now, I ain't a going to do it!"

But, there are those, and may their tribe increase, and may we be among the number counted that increase the crowd, those whose hearts are fixed to *give*. The theological term for that is "grace." And, we would be utterly undone without it. "Man is born broken. He lives by mending. The grace of God is the glue." And man is most like God when he furnishes, or becomes, most "glue."

There is nothing in life that is more moving to see than a great heart firmly fixed in giving. The steward, Matthew, in *A Man For All Seasons,* is impressed by a goblet that Sir Thomas Moore has given to Rich. Musing upon the fact the steward says that his master, Sir Thomas, would give anything he has to anyone. There is difference in opinion as to whether that is good or bad, some think it is good, some think it is bad, but he thinks that Sir Thomas cannot help it. His heart is fixed that way. However, Matthew is afraid that one day someone will ask for something that Sir Thomas wants to keep and he will be "out of practice."

The "practice" is usually at the other end; we require practice in giving, not in witholding. The need is most urgent at the point of the continuing, day to day giving, too. Life shows that most men are capable of a sharp, quick burst of heroic giving in an emergency. It is the day to day "price of eggs," as Mrs. Darnley in, *The Last Puritan,* would say. These are the things that "ruin a woman's life."

How can a person *keep* his heart fixed to give like that? If only one could answer from experience! Instead, it is by faith in God and a certain amount of observation of those who have approached the ideal. The New Testament talks about a "new birth" and "a new man" and "a new creation." It has much to say about "being in Christ" and about "Christ in you the hope of glory." That is our only hope. For certainly this thing of keeping one's heart fixed to give is more than any man can accomplish on his own.

NOTES

1. Used by permission of Max Freedom Long, Huna Research Publications, Vista, California, 1955.

11

"HOME FOR CHRISTMAS"

Lloyd Douglas once wrote a short story that he called, "Home For Christmas." It concerns the Clayton family, five children, two boys and three girls. As children they had grown up in an old-fashioned farmhouse with its accompanying simple life, great joys, and attendant hardships. But long ago they had left the old home and become prosperous American citizens. At the time of the story, Jim and Fred, the two boys in the family, have already made their mark and wealth, while the two older girls have married well and now presided over their homes of ease and affluence. One of the girls, Nan, the youngest, is still single.

Nan has kept the old homestead just as it had been when the Claytons were young. It is her idea that they all go back to the old home place for Christmas to live for a few days just as they had done in their childhood, remembering the hardships and pleasures of those far-off days.

The project sounded a bit alarming to her older brothers and sisters, settled in their comfortable ways, but they were fond of Nan and wished to humor her; so, each agreed to the idea. Plans were made; the in-laws and children were banished and the five Claytons gathered, by themselves, in the old farmhouse. What follows makes a lovely story filled with gentle humor and tender nostalgia all intertwined with two delightful love stories.

Jim and Fred want some old fashion country sausage. The only way they can have it is to kill a pig, which they proceed to do. They wind up mopping the pig, all over the back porch, steps, yard, and smokehouse. Then follows the grinding of the sausage in an old fashioned food chopper; the smell of sage and red pepper is tantalizing! The girls bake the cakes and pies; they roast the nuts, pop the corn, and hang the greens. The boys go to the forest for the Christmas tree and drag it home through the deep snow. The neighbors with whom the Claytons grew up but whom they have not seen for a long time are invited to the home on Christmas Eve for an evening of entertainment.

The occasion is presided over by Miss Packer, a retired school teacher, who has taught almost everyone in the community including the five Claytons. It is a time of happy memories, half-forgotten games, wholesome laughter, home-prepared refreshments. The evening comes to a close with "Packy" calling on Jim Clayton to "speak a few words." Jim was caught off guard; he couldn't turn this into a joke. He stood, looked at the group that he had "loved long since and lost for awhile," and began. He reminded the group of the simple faith loved and cherished by their parents, most of whom had entered the eternal rest—that if all the composers of all time were to meet in conclave it would probably be the unanimous conclusion that of all the immortal songs the anthems of peace chanted one night above the plains of Bethlehem had stirred mankind to its best endeavors; while, the star they remembered hearing about as children had furnished men and women their most luminous ideas.

And one comes to the end of the story with the definite feeling that to be better off does not necessarily mean that one is better, and many of us, along with the Claytons, would do well to go home for Christmas.

It would be difficult to find a word picture that more adequately suggests what Christmas really is than this phrase, "Home for Christmas." Home where the heart is, home where peace and goodwill are, home where warm sentiment and tender love reside, home where God is recognized. No wonder the lovely song, "I'll Be Home For Christmas," is revived each year with its haunting suggestions of snow and mistletoe, presents "on the tree," the place where "lovelight gleams."

It is not just a sense of nostalgia and lost innocence; it is much more than that. It is a great theological fact: mankind is away from home, and evil is responsible. We are told that at 11:30 on the morning of November 20, 1967, America's population reached two hundred million persons. Yet, the figure had to be an estimate, for with all the care and great expense to which the government had gone in taking the census, the census was inaccurate. At least six million people were not counted. Why? *They were away from home!* The census takers could not find them; at least six million people were lost.

In a deeper sense even more millions are away from home. The Scriptures are very sure of this. And, it is not a new condition; it is an ancient problem. It begins with our distant parents, Adam and Eve. They were away from home when God came to visit them; disobedience was the villain. Cain, their son, was driven from home; evil was responsible. Jacob fled from his home and his brother's face; greed was accountable. Joseph was taken from his home and sold as a slave in Egypt; wickedness did it. The prodigal son left his father's house to wander in a "far country;" rebellion prompted him. "Judas went out and it was night;" sin was the culprit. While the ancient prophet lays the charge on the doorstep of the world, "We have turned everyone to his own way."

Man *feels* that he is failing someone or something; he *feels* alienated, isolated, alone, barren, unproductive, wasteful. And, no matter where he goes, no matter what he does, there is the haunting question like that of little Petterkin in "The Battle of Blenheim" by Robert Southy, "But what came of it all at last?" And the echo comes back that it is unknown what came of it all but, "Twas a famous victory. So, man goes on using hands that fashion and heads that know, but his heart, he knows, was lost long, long ago.

This note is repeatedly sounded in modern literature. Behrman's, *Rain From Heaven* has Rand saying that there is some awful fence in his mind and in his spirit and that no matter what

he does he will never be able to break through it. Violet
responds, "We're all shut behind our little fences." Tennessee
Williams in *Orpheus Descending* contends that everyone is sentenced to solitary confinement inside his own skin for life.
Rachel Crothers in, *When Ladies Meet* has Mary say that her
problem is just that no one belongs to her, no one's very
existence depends upon her. She says that she is "completely
and absolutely alone." And the prophet Isaiah asks the disturbing question, "Wherefore do you spend money for that which is
not bread? and your labour for that which satisfieth not?" You
see, man is away from home. That is his problem.

Now, Christmas is God's warm, urgent, ever insistent invitation to his wayward children to come home, *home for Christmas*. The invitation is wrapped in flesh, the flesh of a tiny baby.
This is the best and surest way to send an invitation. Not the
U. S. Mail Service. That service is proficient but if you want to
use life's most effective means of extending an invitation you will
wrap the invitation in a person and send that. It is an expensive
process. You do not always get the speediest reply. Suffering is
often involved. But, for a sure thing, you can do no better than
to use this form of communication. It is the form that God used.

It is said that Francis E. Clark had the word "Welcome"
carved on the beams of his front porch in seventeen different
languages. Excellent! But, it has also been said, by those who
have paid the price of counting, that the word *come* appears
more than six hundred times in the Bible. If the Bible has been
translated in whole or part in more than eleven hundred languages, think of how often God has issued his invitation. And,
originally, the invitation is always wrapped in a person.

Consider a few of the wordings of that invitation. "Thou shalt
call his name Jesus: for he shall save his people from their
sins"; *Home for Christmas!* ". . . They shall call his name
Emmanuel, which being interpreted is, God with us"; *Home for
Christmas!* "For God so loved the world, that he gave his only
begotten Son"; *Home for Christmas!* "But when the fulness of

time was come, God sent forth his Son"; *Home for Christmas!*
"God was in Christ reconciling the world unto himself, no
longer holding men's misdeeds against them" (NEB); *Home for
Christmas!* "The Spirit and the bride say, Come. And let him
that heareth say, Come. And let him that is athirst come. And
whosoever will, let him take the water of life freely." Come—
Home for Christmas! This is God's invitation to all men who are
homesick and who lay their heads in foreign lands when the day
is done.

This is what Christmas is all about. This is its deepest meaning. This is why Christ came. He came as God's warm, urgent
invitation, wrapped in human flesh, inviting men, all men, to
come home for Christmas. The invitation says that all will be
forgiven. The invitation bears an urgent "RSVP." The prophet
saw this centuries ago; Handel's *Messiah* has made it familiar to
the world,

> "Comfort ye, comfort ye my people, saith your God. Speak ye
> comfortably to Jerusalem, and cry unto her, that her warfare is ac-
> complished, that her iniquity is pardoned: for she hath received of
> the Lord's hand double for all her sins."

Let it be put in a quaint and tender story. The story appeared
in a book, now long out of print, that was first published around
the turn of the century called, *Beside The Bonnie Brier Bush* by
Ian Maclaren. Some of the language is now archaic and the tone
is of a different day, but the spirit and the truth are eternal. Let
the story speak for itself.

Lachlan Campbell was a little man, with a spare, wiry body,
iron gray hair and whiskers carefully arranged. His face was
keen and sharpened by much spiritual thinking; he had eyes that
looked at you from beneath shaggy eyebrows as from some
other world; in some ways his face suggested that of a Skye
terrier dog, the most serious of all animals. Lachlan was a
shepherd by trade, but his life's business was theology. He was
an elder in the little Scotish kirk, and he ruled it with an iron

hand. He was sharp, hard, and unbending. No one questioned his sincerity, but all feared his unsmiling Calvinism. He lived alone with his daughter Flora; his wife, Flora's mother, having died at the birth of the child.

Lachlan had tried to be father and mother in his hard, unbending, autocratic way.

There came the day when he stood in the church session and said: "Mr. Moderator, I have to bring a case of discipline before the Session, and ask them to do their duty. It is known to me that a young woman who has been a member of this church has left her home and gone into the far country. There will be no use in summoning her to appear before the Session, for she will never be seen again in this parish. I move that she be cut off from the roll, and her name is," and Lachlan's voice broke, but in an instant he recovered himself—"her name is Flora Campbell."

The minister followed Lachlan home and said, "Lachlan, tell me about it as you would were I your son and Flora's brother." Lachlan handed him a letter.

The preacher read:

Dear Father, When this reaches you I will be in London, and not worthy to cross your door. Do not be always angry with me, and try to forgive me, you will not be troubled anymore by my dancing and my dressing. Do not think that I will be blaming you, for you have been a good father to me, and said what you would be considering right, but it is not easy for a man to understand a girl. Oh, if I had had my mother, then she would have understood me, and I would not have crossed you. Forget poor Flora's foolishness but do not forget her, and maybe you will still pray for me. Take care of the geraniums for my sake, and give milk to the lamb that you called after me. I will never see you again, in this world or the next, nor my mother . . . (here the letter was much blotted). When I think that there will be no one to look after you, and have the fire burning for you on winter nights, I will be rising to come back. But it is too late, too late. Oh, the disgrace I will be bringing on you in the glen.—Your unworthy daughter, Flora Campbell.

The preacher said, "This is a fiery trial, Lachlan, and I cannot even imagine what you are suffering. But, do not despair, for that is not the letter of a bad girl. Perhaps she was impatient, and has been led astray. But Flora is good at heart, and you must not think that she is gone forever."

Lachlan groaned, tottered to his feet and said, "You are kind, Maister Charmichael, but you do not understand." He caught hold of a chair and looked the minister in the face, "She has gone, and there will be no coming back. You would not take her name from the church and I will not be meddling with that book. But I have blotted out her name from my Bible, where her mother's name is written and mine. She has wrought confusion in an elder's house, and I . . . I have no daughter. But I loved her; she never knew how I loved her, for her mother looked at me from her eyes."

They were all helpless until one day Margaret Howe, the sainted woman of the community, met Lachlan in the village and saw how he was dying of heartache. She went to see him and was welcomed as only a Scot knows how to welcome a guest. She came directly to the point. "Maister Campbell," she said, "you will believe me that I have come in the love of God, and because we have both been afflicted. I had a son and he is gone. I know where George is and am satisfied. I do not doubt that your sorrow is greater than mine."

"Would to God she was lying younder in the kirkyard; but I will not speak of her. She is not anything to me this day. See, I will show you what I have done, for she has been a black shame to her name." He opened the Bible, and there was Flora's name scored, marked throughout with wavering strokes, but the ink had run as if it had been mingled with tears. Margaret's heart burned within her at the sight, and she could scarcely make allowance for Lachlan's blood and theology.

She flamed, "This is what you have done, and you let a woman see your work! You are an old man and in sore trial, but I tell you before God you have the greater shame. Just twenty years this spring and her mother died. No woman to watch over her, and she wandered from the fold, and all you can do is to take her name out of your Bible. What if our heavenly Father had blotted out our name from the Book of Life when we left his house? But he sent his dear Son to seek us, and a weary road he came . . . I tell you, a man would not leave a sheep to perish as you have cast off your own child. You are worse than Simon the Pharisee, for Mary was no kin to him. Poor Flora, to have such a father."

It was a sharp arrow, but an arrow that found its mark. Lachlan softened and Margaret wrote a letter for she now knew that it would be well with Lachlan. This is what she wrote to Flora:

My Dear Lassie, You know that I was always your friend, and I am writing this to say that your father loves you more than ever, and is a wearing his heart out for the sight of his child. Come back or he will die for the want of your face. The glen is bright and bonnie now, for the purple heather is on the hills, and down below the golden corn, with the blue bells and the poppy flowers in between. Nobody will ask you where you've been, or anything else; there's not a child in the place that is not wearing to see your face. And, Flora, if there will be much gladness in our wee glen when ye come home, what think ye of the joy in the Father's house? So, start the very minute you get this letter; your father bids you come, and I'm writing this in the place of your mother."

Margaret took the letter to Lachlan to read; he addressed it with his own hand. He went with Margaret as far as the brow of the hill. When he returned he put the big light in the window to burn until Flora came.

It was night when Flora got off the train at the little station a mile or so from her father's house. When she came in sight of the house she saw the light. At first she feared that her father was ill; then it dawned upon her that maybe the light was for her. She ran and fell exhausted against the door; she had no strength to knock or breath to call but the dogs heard and recognized. They set up such a joyous howl that Lachlan recognized her, too. He fumbled at the latch until he got the door open. Then her father, who in his sternness had never kissed her, stopped the speech that she had ready to make, all she got to say was, "Father." And all her father could say was "Flora, Flora."

Later she told Margaret about it. She said, "It is a pity that you do not know Gaelic; it is the best of languages for loving. There are fifty words for darling and my father was using all of them the night I came home." "O Margaret," she continued, "the Lord has had mercy upon me; for the rest I shall be saying to him."

"But," interrupted Lachlan, "there is something that I must say and it is not easy." He brought the Bible and opened it at the family register where her name had been and was erased. "Will you ever be able to forgive me?" he said. "Give me the pen, Margaret;" Flora wrote for a minute while Lachlan never raised his head. She gave him the Book and this is what he read:

Flora Campbell
Missed April 1873
Found September 1873

Her father fell on her neck and kissed her.

That, you see, is what Christmas means! It means *Home For Christmas!*

Come, let us rise and go home to the Father.

12

"ON MAKING COVENANTS"

We stand on the threshold of a New Year. We look back and we look forward. There is much in the backward look that brings regret; the forward look is a mixture of fear and hope. Where may we turn for courage and strength?

This discussion suggests that help may be found in giving thought to a good man who had a bad father. The good man's name was Hezekiah; the bad father's name was Ahaz. The names are not especially important, what their lives represented is.

The father worshipped pagan gods, built altars to them, burned incense to them, and even gave one of his own sons as a human sacrifice. He allowed the church of the living God to be closed and the building to fall into disrepute. The law of holy God was forgotten; wickedness was abroad in high and in low places. This was the condition of things when the son, the good man, came to the throne. "If the foundations be destroyed what can the righteous do?"

Two things. The righteous can be righteous and the righteous can rebuild the foundations. That is exactly what this good man did. He made no excuses; there was no waiting for conditions to improve. He opened the doors of the house of God. The lamps in the house of God, the symbol of learning, were relit. He called for dedicated and aggressive leadership on the part of the clergy. He confessed his own failures and the failures of his people. He made worthy offerings in the house of God. He courageously analyzed the civil and political conditions in his country. And he made a covenant with God.

That is the first thing he did; the covenant had priority. He said, "Now it is in my heart to make a covenant with the Lord God of Israel." A covenant is a voluntary agreement arrived at by two or more people. Here it was a pledge, a promise, in which God bound himself with the young man, and the young man bound himself to God. It was a free binding of each to the other, based upon certain conditions. "Now it is in my heart," said the young king, "to make a covenant with the Lord." The covenant is an explanation of the young man's resolution, his moral indignation, and his spiritual sensitivity.

This is the New Year season, a time for looking back, a time for facing forward. It is a time for confession of failures experienced in the past year; it is a time for resolutions and commitments for the year ahead. It is a time for covenant-making. Never underestimate the important covenants, covenants made with one's better self, with his fellows and most important of all, covenants made with one's God.

Covenants serve as monuments and memorials. See. Life begins with ideals; the youthful spirit sees to that. "We hope, we aspire, we resolve, we trust when the morning calls us to life and light." Yes, but go on with the rest of the lines, "But our hearts grow weary, and, ere the night, our lives are trailing the sordid dust." The attrition of the days, the months, and the years take their toll.

Robert Robinson was converted through the preaching of George Whitefield. When Robinson was twenty he heard John Wesley; it was the preaching of Wesley that led him to become a minister. Two years later, when he was twenty-two and pastor at Norwich, Robinson wrote the hymn, "Come Thou Fount of Every Blessing, tune my heart to sing Thy grace." Years later, when trials and discouragement had done their stint to his faith, a woman reproved him for his waywardness and read to him the words of his own hymn. "Madam," he is said to have replied, "I am the poor, unhappy man who composed it; and I would give a thousand worlds, if I had them, to enjoy the feelings I knew then."

It is often at this point that a covenant does its work. We come upon it as a lover might come upon a long lost keepsake. Then memory begins to bless and to burn. The covenant says: "When you made this covenant with the Lord you thought this way; you felt in this manner; you said this and this and this; you did this and that. What about it? Look at you now! Did you mean it then or do you mean it now? Are you going to repudiate all that now and forget the whole matter? Possibly you would like to renew that covenant today, right here, right now. What about it?"

In *The Big Fisherman,* Lloyd Douglas pictures Jesus' healing of Simon Peter's mother-in-law, Hannah. A young Arab girl, Fara, loves Hannah and has been led to pray for her recovery. As the girl leaves the room to prepare food for Hannah after the miracle, Jesus speaks sharply to her. "If you have made a new promise today, see that you keep it! God is not mocked!" And you?

It was so with Charles Kingsley. One evening walking by the sea the covenant making, and the covenant keeping God became very real to Kingsley as the thought of all that might have been and was not. Going to his room he made the following entry in his journal: "My birthnight! Before the sleeping earth and the sleeping stars I have devoted myself to God; a vow, never again, if he gives me the faith I pray for, to be recalled." And that was that! It is a ministry of covenants. They stand as memorials and call us back to better things. They demand that we keep our promises.

Here is a second thing that covenants do for us. They stand as milestones to mark our progress or the lack of it. For often it is not a matter of completely forsaking our "first love" but a slow cooling of it. The covenant is made and time flees. Life takes its pound of flesh, and more seriously, its ounce of the Holy Grail. Somehow, "new occasions teach new duties," and new compromises. Time makes so much of "ancient good uncouth." New conditions, new circumstances, new morals brainwash us. And then we are brought face to face with an old covenant.

It may be that we had written it down—sealed it in an envelope; an envelope now yellow through time—to be opened and read at a certain date. It may have been written on the fly-leaf of an old Bible—and that too, has been forgotten—now it is read again.

Or friends remember and say as they said to Peter in the courtyard, "Did I not see thee in the garden with him?" or in the baptismal waters, or in the choir, or in the Sunday School class, or in the retreat high in the hills of commitment? Then, why are you here where I see you now?

The confrontation demands a progress report. That can be a devastating thing! Am I as close to Christ and his will for my life as I was ten years ago? Do I trust him as much now as I did then? Am I as eager that his will be realized in my life and work now as I desired it then? Do I obey his leading now as I sought to obey it then? Am I as sincere in my efforts to make him known now as I was then? Am I as ambitious to serve the unfortunate, to give the "cup of cold water" now as then? With the psalmist, do I love his house now as then? His kingdom? If I can honestly say that I love God as much now as then, there is still another question that must be answered. It is this: Do I hate evil as much as I hated it then? The psalmist emphasized both needs, "Ye who love the Lord," he said, "hate evil." It is dreadfully easy for our sense of values to become warped.

Lloyd Douglas in, *Time to Remember,* tells about a letter that his brother Clyde once received from Sam Logan, a boyhood friend. The letter read:

"Dear Clyde, How are you? Well, I hope. We are alright here. Do you still have the white rat? Mind that pair of rabbits I had? I have sold lots of rabbits. School has took up again. I hate school.

Your friend,
Sam Logan

P.S. Pap died last night."

But the covenant becomes a milestone. We see just where we are in relationship to where we were when the covenant was made. And it may, by God's grace, cause us to become pilgrims again.

It was this way with Jacob, remember? Jacob had grown old and rich. The cares and the anxieties of life had crowded in upon him. God said, "Go back to Bethel." It was at Bethel that Jacob had camped his first night away from home, when he was fleeing from his brother. How long ago it all seemed; how much had transpired! That long ago experience came back to him now as the voice of God echoed in his soul, "Back to Bethel."

Jacob remembered how in that long ago he had fled across the burning sands, how he cast a glance over his shoulder every few minutes to see if he was being followed by his angry brother. Tired, lonely, afraid, Jacob kept his pace until the burning sun went down. Then among the rocks he found a hiding place, taking one of the stones for a pillow, he fell into a deep sleep. That night he dreamed he saw a ladder reaching from earth to heaven. On the ladder were angels. They were going up and they were coming down. From the top of the ladder God spoke to him. It was a vivid experience; it seemed so real!

When the youth awoke he cried, "God was in this place and I knew it not . . . this is the house of God, and this is the gate of Heaven." So, Jacob set up his monument and there he made his covenant with God. But Jacob had not been dilligent in keeping his part of the covenant. Now, at the bidding of God, he makes his preparation to return to his covenant-making place. He says to his family and his servants, "Dedicate yourselves; get rid of our idols; tomorrow we go back to Bethel where God appeared to me in my youth." The memory of that covenant was a milestone for Jacob.

Covenants do a third thing for us. They act as stabilizers. Some high hour when life is good and God is near and his will and purpose are plain we make a covenant. We take our reading and we know that the reading is correct. Later the clouds form; the sea roars, heaves, and foams, but we hold our course because we trust the earlier readings.

"In every life," says Tournier in *The Seasons of Life,* "there are few special moments that count for more than all the rest because they mean the taking of a stand, a self-commitment, a decisive choice. It is commitment that creates the person. It is by commitment that man reveals his humanity."

Life needs that sort of thing. The skies are not always clear; God does not seem always near; his will and purpose are not always discernible. But, there are times of truth. It is wisdom to trust the vision of these best hours not the worst, to remain true to the covenants made in those shining hours, and not rely upon the moods experienced during the "dark night of the soul." A man like the prophet Elijah has to make a choice. He can believe the reality of the fire falling from heaven and consuming the altar, or he can believe his fear when he is fleeing from Jezebel; he cannot live by both. John the Baptist can believe his insight and his vision when he cries, "Behold the lamb of God that taketh away the sin of the world." Or, he may rely on his doubts that cry, "Art thou he that should come, or do we look for another?" He cannot stake his life on both. Neither can you or I. Which shall it be?

Surely, it is the point of wisdom to believe our best hours, to act upon the insights, the resolutions formed, the covenants made when life was at its clearest. After he finished his "Dream of Gerontius," Sir Edward Elgar wrote to a friend saying that this was the best thing that he had ever done. He said that for the rest he ate and drank and slept and loved and hated like other men. Then he wrote, ". . . but this I saw and knew; this, if anything of mine, is worth your memory." Now, would it not be wise for Sir Edward to believe *that,* not the hours when he was "like another?"

Possibly you remember the scene in *Jane Eyre,* when Rochester is pleading with Jane to go away with him to the south of France. They love each other; all Jane's life she has dreamed of such a love. Rochester's pleadings are almost irresistible. Only the memory, the vision, the ideals, only what she had covenanted in her soul saved her; but, save her it did. She said, and it is one of the shining words in literature:

"I care for myself. The more solitary, the more friendless, the more unstained I am, the more I will respect myself. I will keep the law given by God; sanctioned by man. I will hold the principles received by me when I was sane and not mad as I am now. Laws and principles are not for the time when there are no temptations; they are for such moments as this; when body and soul rise in mutiny against their rigor. Stringent they are; inviolate they shall be. If at my individual conscience I could break them, what would be their worth—so I have always believed and if I cannot believe it now, it is because I am insane; with my veins running fire, and my heart beating faster than I can count its throb. *Here I plant my foot.*

There you have it. "So I have believed . . . If I cannot believe it now it is because I am insane . . . Here I plant my foot!" You have to believe your good hours or your bad hours, which shall it be? One of them is a lie. Where do you plant your foot?

13

"MARK THE EARTH
WITH A CROSS"

It is fearfully easy to forget great events and to live as if they had never occurred. So Bernard Shaw realizes in *St. Joan.* One who voted for Joan's death afterwards confesses that it was an awful thing that he had done, a cruel thing, but that he never really knew what cruelty was like until he saw a young girl burned to death. The Bishop asks, "Must then a Christ perish in torment in every age to save those that have no imagination?"

In his play, *Valley Forge,* Maxwell Anderson has George Washington to say, as he surveys his starving, freezing, dwindling recruits, "Men will think lightly of this liberty when they forget what it cost." "Hard to remember, easy to forget." In *Family Portrait,* the authors have Mary to ask one of her sons, for her sake, to give the name Jesus to his newly born baby, "Because," she says, "it is a good name, and I would not want that it be forgotten."

Fearfully easy to forget great events and to live as if they never occurred!

On Monument Avenue in Richmond, Virginia, along with many other statues, is the monument of General Robert E. Lee, soldier, statesman, educator, Christian gentleman. Thousands pass the monument every day without so much as a lifted eye. But, a friend of mine told me how he once drove past that statue with Dr. John R. Sampey, the Hebrew scholar. When they came to within a block of the statue Dr. Sampey became silent; then he said, "Is that the statue of General Lee?" My friend assured him that it was. Immediately, Dr. Sampey sat at attention, made a sharp salute, held the salute until they were well past the monument, then at ease again, the old man said, in a husky voice, "My hero!" "Hard to remember, easy to forget."

Or, in Washington, our capital city, you walk in the area of the Lincoln Memorial. You seldom go that you do not see a group of school children, led and lectured by their teacher. The children are quiet, their faces are upturned, and in their eyes is the glow of adoration. Yet, look closely and unless the park workman have done their work within the last few hours, you will see trash, filth, cigarette butts, beer bottles, and cans at the base of the monument.

At the death of the Kennedys and the Kings we are deeply moved. We vow that never again shall hatred and prejudice and violence have any place with us. But, within a few short weeks we are thinking, saying, acting as those dark and dreadful crimes were never committed. "Hard to remember, easy to forget."

It is frightfully easy to forget Calvary and to live as if that event had never taken place. There are, of course, times when we do become conscious of the truth. It may be at some quiet Communion service when the bread and the wine are given as emblems of Christ's sacrifice, or it may be at some high hour of dedication and commitment when the tides of the Spirit are running high and young lives are deeply moved and freely offered. But the fogs close in; the horizons narrow; indifference and selfishness becomes the order of the day again, and we forget and go on living as if that event never took place.

Following the crucifixion life moved on in Jerusalem, no doubt, about as it had before. There was the same bartering and haggling in the market place; the same shrewd financial deals in the places of exchange; things went on in about the same way in the homes. There was not much change in people's attitude toward God and men, toward the sacred and the holy. Anatole France, the brilliant French writer, pictures Pilate as an old man talking to a friend. The friend mentions the crucifixion of Jesus. He says, "Pontus, do you remember anything about the man?"

After a long and thoughtful pause, Pilate answers, "Jesus? Jesus —of Nazareth? I cannot call him to mind."

The great Scot preacher, Arthur John Gossip, in *The Hero In Thy Soul* thinks that there was one man in that crucifying mob, however, who did remember and who never did forget; his name was Simon of Cyrene. He came into the city from the country just as the mob was moving toward Calvary. He saw the crowd, was curious, and moved toward it. Just as he got to it, the Master fell beneath the weight of his cross. The Roman soldier looked about him for help. His eyes rested on Simon. There he was; tall, broad shouldered, sure of himself. The soldier ordered Simon to carry the cross to the top of the hill. Simon immediately protested. He had nothing to do with the degrading business; he was a stranger in the city, had just arrived; he was there on legitimate business; it was time for his appointment; he simply had to be on his way. But, the soldier was accustomed to being obeyed; he was the authority. So Simon became a conscript cross-bearer.

Simon was angry and humiliated. He swore his vengeance upon the soldier and the Roman system that the soldier represented. Simon would never forget or forgive the insult. He would get even if it was the last thing he ever did. Or, if Simon became a Christian, and the New Testament indicates that he did, he would remember the incident in another vein and spirit, but no less vividly. In the act of sin or weakness he would burn with repentance. "Holy God," he would cry, "must I forever wound him whom I adore. Was it not enough that I should assist in his crucifixion? Must I forever go on with the wounding?" Or, if, on another day, he was challenged and moved to perform some task of extraordinary devotion and sacrifice, the long ago event would be vividly in his mind, and he would cry, "Blessed be this privilege! Once more I am permitted to make his task a little lighter by participating in his suffering. Once in the long ago, by God's grace, I was allowed to make the hill of Calvary a little less severe; now, again, the privilege is mine.

Most gladly will I perform this deed in his name." And, so by acts great and small, by service that was easy and service that called for sacrifice, Simon kept that great event fresh in his mind and heart.

And that is how it has to be done if it is to be done at all. Let us never neglect nor depreciate the hours of quiet and sacred worship. We shall be utterly undone if we do. But, ultimately, the only way to keep the cross of Christ vividly before us, fresh within us so that it can perform its task through us, is to take up our own cross and go marching off after him. For the cross of Calvary is not primarily a thing to be adored but a life giving truth to be lived. It must become a very part of the lives we live; it must be ground into the very soil and substance of our existence; its spirit and power must overshadow, undergird, overarch every act of life. It needs to become the standard by which we measure our own lives, action and everything about us.

There was an old legend that said it was never safe to die until one had taken a stick and marked on the earth the sign of the cross. Legend and superstition? Of course, and yet! As is so often the case, a legend based upon a great truth. For until we mark the earth, our work, our lives, our influence, with the cross, we can neither live nor die rightly. Run that truth out into life and see its relevancy.

Take the matter of evil, evil in our personal lives. Do we dare to mark that with the cross? There was a time when these disturbed us, when conscience put up a loud howl about it, when we even shed tears about it, went to the "lonesome valley" over it, spent time in trying to eradicate it from our lives. We did what Robert Louis Stevenson once called, "Hewing Agag to pieces." But now, that seems old fashioned, completely out of date and style. Everyone acts this way, submits, yields, succumbs to these things, why worry about it! Circumstances called for such action.

Somewhere Maeterlink pictures God sitting on the sunny side

of a green hill smiling at man's offences as a man might smile at
his puppy playing on a rug before an open fire. That, I know, is
repulsive; if we have any traditional theological upbringing the
idea is utterly revolting. Yet, I challenge my own heart and I
challenge yours. Before we completely banish that awful picture
from our minds let us have the courage to do a little soul
searching. What do we care about a selfish spirit; how disturbed
are we over outbursts of temper? How conscious stricken are we
over prejudice; when were we deeply concerned because of
greed, covetousness, and lust? When did a cry arise from our
soul begging God to remove an unforgiving spirit?

Or, again, take the slow seepage of the world's spirit to our
lives. The apostle Paul cautioned, "Be not conformed to this
world: but be ye transformed by the renewing of your mind."
There is a tendency among us to reverse the Pharisee's prayer.
He prayed, "God, I thank thee, that I am not as other men."
See how we pray it. "I thank thee, Lord, that I am as other
men." Nothing is different for us. We want to be "good guys,"
"regular fellows," "one of the gang." I know that there is a
"separateness" that is unchristian; I know that we can withdraw
from the world and act as if we were more holy than Christ, for
he did not isolate himself from the world. Let us never forget
however, that in being *where they were* did not mean for Christ
being *as they were*. It was because he was different that he went
where they were. He went to help, to redeem; he went with the
curative point of view. Had he become one with the world's
"slow stain" he would have been unable to help. It does no good
for a doctor to contract the disease of his patient. We do not
help a delinquent by deliberately placing ourselves in the position to contract his venereal disease to show him that we care
about his condition.

Mark that section of life with the cross and we shall see that
in order to be helpful we must not be conformed, we must be
renewed. A woman told her neighbor, and with great pride, "I
must get to church early today; our Johnny is going to be

conformed." But, Matthew Arnold once wrote of another poet, "From the contagion of the world's slow stain, he is secure." We need that security.

Or, again, think of the evil that is the condition of others. How long has it been since their condition really disturbed us. There was a time when it did. And, that disturbance was on very good authority. Jesus wept over Jerusalem and cried, "How oft I would . . . but, you would not." And because of that "would not" tragic circumstances lay ahead.

James Stewart in *Thine is the Kingdom,* lists five basic motives that have moved the churches to evangelistic and missionary endeavor. They are: Commission, Compassion, Community, Continuity, and Christ. We have all but forgotten the first two; we give lip-service to the fifth; the third and fourth are often so reinterpreted that they mean little. Hal Luccock once wrote of the man who wired his publishers: "How much advance will you give for a novel of 60,000 words." Back came a wire from the publisher asking another question. "How big are the words?" In eagerness to communicate with the world we have adopted a different vocabulary, almost totally different vocabulary. Up to a point, of course, that is good. The gospel now, as then, needs to be so preached that every man can hear it in his own language. However, it must be the *gospel* that is preached. It is impossible to change the entire language of the Bible, tradition and Christian doctrine, without changing the content of the gospel. The language of the psychiatrist, psychologist, physician, consultant in mental disorders does not easily carry the weight contained in biblical and theological terms. Of course, some one might ask, "since when did these 'professionals' worry about the 'average' man understanding their jargon!"

The plain truth is, we no longer are disturbed by the sinful plight of men. That is too sweeping a statement, of course; there are those who do care, and care mightily. But, it is a generalization for which much support can be mustered. And, if we still wish to make any appreciable use of the Bible, we simply must care about the spiritual condition of men. John Woleman wrote in his Journal: "I felt the depth and extent of the misery of my fellow creatures, separated from the divine harmony, and it was greater than I could bear, and I was crushed down under it."

That is to say, mark the sinful condition of men, all men, who are without Christ, mark them with the cross and their condition will concern us. When Donald Fraser, the great hearted missionary came home from his outstanding service in Central Africa, the natives sent him a message of thanks. In it they sought to recount what he had done for them. He had, they said, found them savages, and had left them immeasurably enriched, he had lifted them far above, centuries above, where they had stood when he came; he had given them schools and churches; he had led them into fellowship with Christ. They closed the account with a sentence that deserves to live among all who would mark their work with the cross. They said, "We are ashamed we have not caught the infection of a like heart."

Look again and try to mark another area with the cross, mark the physical, the material, the bodily needs and circumstances of men. For it is the whole man that Christ came to minister to, not a half—part man. The fact that we all too often lose sight of man's spiritual need, and we do, gives us no ground for neglecting the rest of man. A. A. Milne wrote some beautiful nursery verses that our children loved. One of them told about being "halfway up the stairs." It points out that "Halfway up the stairs isn't up and it isn't down. It isn't in the nursery and it isn't town." No, it isn't. And, it is easy to be just "halfway up and halfway down" in our commitment to men through our love for Christ.

When the disciples came to Jesus reminding him that he was overlooking the physical needs of the people, saying that the people were hungry, that they had been listening to him preach all day, there and then those disciples learned a lesson. They learned a lesson about the concern of Jesus for the whole man. He said, "They need not depart; give ye them to eat." As if to say, "It is not my oversight; it is your lack of concern that is at fault. I shall not send the people away to seek material needs as you wish me to do; it is your business to meet those physical needs; of course the people must be fed."

There may be, indeed there is, ground for careful consideration of the place of the churches in cooperating with community, state, and national agencies to meet the needs of the people. If the world is in the churches, and it is, the churches need to be in the world, though not "of it." The churches must keep their windows open toward Jerusalem, otherwise they are lame like the beggar at the pool; but, unless the churches keep their doors open to the street they deny their Lord who said, "They need not depart; you give them to eat." Let us mark that with a cross.

Aye, it is fearfully easy to forget great events and to live as if they never occurred. The only way to avoid it is to mark all of life, not just a part of it, with the cross. Let me show you, in a poignant story, told in *The Apostles' Creed for Everyman* by William Barclay, just what that means. Once Sir George Adam Smith, the great Old Testament scholar found as his seat-mate on a train a young missionary who was going out to the foreign field. The young man was tall and handsome, winsome and attractive, brilliant and gifted; this was all soon evident as they talked together. The young man told Dr. Smith that he was going to a part of Africa where, at that time, a white man's life was measured not in terms of years but of months. The climate, the disease were simply more than the body could stand. There were no medicines and inoculations available. Even though George Adam Smith was a Christian scholar the young man's undertaking seemed a waste of life and talent and ability. He tried to reason with the young missionary; surely there was some other place of significant service where he might invest his great abilities for a longer period of time and, therefore, for a greater good. But, the young man was firm; to the needy but dangerous lands he must and would go. The train came to the station where Dr. Smith was to depart; and the young missionary was to continue his journey. The older man still tried to reason with the younger man. But, as the train left the station, the young man was in the door of the train, and the last words he heard the young man say were these: "He loved me and gave himself for me—Can I hold anything back?"

14

"LAZARUS LAUGHED"

Suppose you had been dead four days. Now imagine that by some miraculous power you had been brought back to life. How do you think you would view your life? How do you think you would view the life of those around you? How do you think you would react to the way people live, to the circumstances under which they live?

Would you pity the people for their sad plight? Would you scorn them for their ignorance and weakness? Or, would you be angry and impatient with them for their oppression and cruelty? Perhaps you would be moved to compassion because of their confusion and frustration? You could be distressed over their lack of faith in God and his promises? Or, you might be tolerant and amused?

The dramatist Eugene O'Neill seems to think that a bit of each of those moods would be present, but he thinks that more of the last mood would be present. In one of his lesser known plays he sets forth this idea. The title of the play is *Lazarus Laughed*. While it is one of his lesser known plays, O'Neill considered it one of his most representative, and, he arrived at his evaluation on the reaction of his audiences.[1]

The play is based on the raising of Lazarus, the story found in the eleventh chapter of John. The play is a good place to begin an Easter sermon. The first scene takes place in the home of Lazarus in Bethany. It is shortly after Lazarus has been raised from the dead. The father of Lazarus is giving a banquet in honor of his son's return to life.

As the curtain rises Lazarus is seated in the center at a long table. In appearance he is impressive; he is tall, powerfully built; he is about fifty years of age. His face is dark complected, ruddy and brown, the "color of the rich earth is in him." His forehead is broad and noble. His eyes are dark and deep-set. There is a slight halo about his head and from his body is seen a soft illumination as of tiny phosphorescent flames.

A chorus of old men are singing: "Jesus wept; behold how he loved him; he that liveth; he that believeth; shall never die; Lazarus, come forth!" The guests talk and you are allowed to overhear their conversation. They are not unanimous in their opinions. Some are awed; just think of it, four days in the grave! Others are envious and suspicious, did he really die? Was he really dead or did he just *seem* to be dead? There were those who were firm in their assurance, they *saw* the miracle take place; there was just no question about it; the miracle was real. The note of sorrow was uppermost with some; they remembered Lazarus before all this took place; his life had been a disappointment to all; now, this, it all seemed so strange.

The guests talk about the change that has come over Lazarus. He is not the same; he does not look the same; he does not sound the same; he certainly does not act the same. Before there was a look of deep sorrow in his eyes; now there is a deep, dark, ruddy, life-giving glow on his face. His eyes are fountains of joy and peace. Before the miracle he never seemed quite sure about himself, others, or conditions. He was hesitant, he floundered, could never make up his mind or come to definite conclusions. But, now he is sure; he is positive, now his very presence says, "Yes!" Then he was sad; now he is glad. Then he often wept; now he is continually laughing.

Laughter above all else; he is constantly laughing. He laughed when he came out of the tomb. Jesus looked into his eyes for what seemed to be a long time. And then Lazarus suddenly said, "Yes," as if he were answering the question he read in Jesus' eyes. Then Jesus smiled gently as if he were remembering from a distance of former joy.

Lazarus knelt at Jesus' feet; they both smiled, and Jesus

called him, "my brother." The Master turned and walked away; Lazarus watched him go, and began to "laugh softly like a man in love with God."

Others hearing the laughter began to laugh with him. One said, "Such laughter I never heard! It made my ears drunk! And though I was half-dead with fright I found myself laughing too."

This was a characteristic of the laughter of Lazarus, others hearing it laughed, also. Lazarus wanted it that way. He said, "Laugh, laugh with me! Death is dead! Fear is no more. There is only laughter." His house became known as the house of laughter. Workmen come and serve for nothing, only because of laughter; while they sow the fields they dance in the furrows. They sing their songs to the earth as they plow; they lift their faces to the sun and laugh as they tend their flocks on the hillsides.

The soldiers of Caesar come to assassinate Lazarus. The daggers are drawn. Lazarus begins to laugh; the daggers are dropped and the soldiers begin to laugh with him. The galley slaves make music with their chains to the tempo of his laughter. Lazarus said, to the heir of the throne of Rome, "Go out under the sky! Let your heart climb on laughter to a star." So, Lazarus laughed; *why?*

The question is based upon an assumption, of course. The scriptures do not say that Lazarus laughed when he returned from the dead. That is a dramatist's supposition. A case might be made for the supposition. Laughter is not alien to the Scriptures. Sarah said that God had made her to laugh in such a way that all who heard would laugh with her. We are assured that there is a time to laugh and a time to cry. One of the Beatitudes, according to Luke, affirms, "Blessed are ye that weep now: for ye shall laugh." The psalmist said that when their captivity was turned their mouths were filled with laughter. The psalmist also says that God will laugh at the overthrow of evil and the triumph of good. Fullness of life, joy, merriment, completeness, triumph are notes that were sounded by Jesus. Elton Trueblood writes a scholarly book on, *The Humor of Christ. Why* did Lazarus laugh?

Because he had seen life on the other side? All men are curious about that, believers, nonbelievers, pagans, Christians. The first question O'Neill has his neighbors put to Lazarus is this: "What did you find beyond there, Lazarus?" Whatever else the flood of books, magazine articles, consultations, and discussions about the possibility of communicating with the dead may say, and much is being said in our day, they certainly do say that man is curious about the beyond. Questions are asked, questions ranging all the way from the deeply philosophical and theological to the childish and the simple—it may be that what seems most like a child's question is in truth the deepest questions asked. In poetry and music we peer beyond.

To his neighbor's insistant cry for light on the beyond, Lazarus said: "O curious and greedy ones, is not one world in which you know not how to live enough for you." No, it was not enough; it is not enough; it has never been enough. Man was born curious! And, one of the things he is most curious about is the "last things." He may not, he certainly should not, crash a party uninvited in order to have his questions answered, but he will keep on being concerned until he knows as he is known. Leonard Griffith in *The Legacy of the Upper Room* writes of a faithful minister who lay dying, seeing his sorrowing family gathered about the bed, he said, "You mustn't be sad. All my life I have preached to people about the joys of heaven. Now I am going to discover them for myself." To know the answer to questions that have been asked by all men since the dawn of man would be something to laugh about!

Again, Lazarus may well have laughed because, having seen life from the other side he had a new and more perfect evaluation of life on this side. He now saw life from God's point of view, and God's point of view is often different from man's point of view. In writing to the Colossians Paul said, "We are asking God that you may see things, as it were, from his point of view" (Phillips). What a phrase! What a request and possibility to see things from God's point of view! No other view is valid or enduring. Man is constantly changing his view. This is sometimes well, for man's view is partial and imperfect. It was in medicine, in astronomy, in geography; it has often been in theology. Man's view of the child was less than God's view, especially man's view of the girl child. Man's view of his brother has been imperfect; think of the long story of slavery and of race prejudice. Man's view and God's view has been at variance in matters of numbers and size. Then, man should have a spirit of humility and teachableness. Again and again he has found himself doing what Gamaliel said was a real possibility: "You might actually find yourself fighting against God" (Phillips).

O'Neill makes his case, the case is biblical as we have seen, at this point. Lazarus saw that most men were "majoring on minors and minoring on majors." They were setting up required courses that should have been electives, and electives that should have been requirements for any worthy diploma in life's race. He saw that the things that men were afraid of were no real cause for fear. Browning set this idea forth in a poem on Lazarus:

"Should this child," he wrote of Lazarus, "sicken unto death-
     why, look
   For scarce abatement of his cheerfulness,
   Or pretermission of his daily craft!
   While a word, a gesture, a glance from that same child
   At play or in school or laid asleep
   Will startle him to an agony of fear,
   Exasperation just as like."

But basically and fundamentally Lazarus' laughter proceeded from his knowledge that death was dead. We have it on good authority that "death is the final enemy." It is knowledge for "the other side," whether a man has visited there himself, or whether tidings of the place has been given to him by Christ that makes it possible for him to say, "O death, where is thy sting? O grave, where is thy victory? . . . Thanks be to God which giveth us the victory through our Lord Jesus Christ."

Dictators and tyrants have made fearful use of this fear of death, they still do. When Lazarus says to Caligula, the man who is approaching the throne of Rome, "Death is dead, Caligula!" The tyrant cries, "You lie! . . . I say there must be death! . . . You have murdered my only friend, Lazarus! Death would have been my slave when I am Caesar. He would have been my jester and made me laugh at fear!" And, Lazarus answers, "Be your own jester instead, O Caligula! Laugh at yourself, O Caesar-to-be."

Dictators are still making use of the tyrant death. Men yield and submit and confess to all sorts of crimes that they never committed because of their fear of death, fear of death for themselves, and, worse, fear of death to loved ones. It is only when that fear is removed that men can stand tall and walk tall in the face of tyranny, poverty, disease, and oppression.

And so, Lazarus could laugh when he saw the death of his father and mother, his sisters, Martha and Mary, his wife, his followers, and his own death. In the throws of death, with the flames licking at his life he says to Caligula, "Fear not, Caligula! There is no death!"

That is the dramatist view of death. For the Christian, the child of God, it is true, Hear the words of Jesus:

"Jesus said unto her, I am the resurrection, and the life: he that believeth in me, though he were dead, yet shall he live: and whosoever liveth and believeth in me shall never die. Believest thou this? She said unto him, Yea, Lord: I believe."

And you? "Believest thou this?" Can you answer, "Yea, Lord: I believe"?

15

"WHAT'S IN A NAME?"

"It was in Antioch that the disciples first got the name of Christians." (Acts 11:26, NEB) Why? That was their main business and concern; that is how they got the name. Here was a group of people who were following Christ, Christus. They talked Christ. They preached Christ, they taught Christ, they prayed to Christ, they met in Christ's name. As one man was given the name of "Carpenter" because he was a carpenter, so, these "of the way" became "Christians." The name was given in part through scorn, in part through admiration, and, no doubt, in part through mystery, but it was given because of an involvement, a commitment, and a devotion.

It did not mean that these people were not involved in other endeavors; they were. They were bakers, carpenters, smiths, weavers, farmers, and "candlestick makers," but all this was secondary. Their main business was Christ; hence, it was from this source that they derived their name.

Immediately the implications of that bear in upon you. A Christian is one whose main business is Christ! No matter what his other involvements may be, no matter what the profession at which he makes a *living,* he makes a *life* out of following, living, and affirming Jesus Christ. So much so, that if friends and enemies are going to identify him with a *main* concern he has to be identified with Christ. That, though, gives cause for serious attention, does it not? If only those are to be called "Christian" who receive the name on the above qualifications, there would be a thinning and paring down of our numbers! Not only personally, but the idea is disturbing from the standpoint of institutions and groupings. For example, America is called a "Christian nation." The designation is understandable; under certain conditions the designation is legitimate and useful; yet, by the above yardstick, who would call America a Christian nation? What of homes, or schools, or hospitals, or dare we say it, churches?

There is the delightful, if disturbing story of the small boy who felt that he could not go to a certain party because it was his understanding that Christians were not supposed to attend such functions. The boy's minister assured him that he had been misinformed. He should, by all means, attend the function, enjoy it fully. The boy did. Later the minister asked if he had enjoyed the event. The boy's answer was revealing. "Yes! I certainly did have a good time. No one even suspected I was a Christian!"

The word "Christian" or "Christians," appears only three times in the New Testament. Antioch was the first place; it was when the followers of Christ were given their name, given it because of their commitment to Christ. The second time the word is used . . . Well, see the setting.

For two years Paul had been a prisoner in Caesarea. Then a new governor, Festus, by name, took office. Immediately Paul's old enemies came forth to accuse him before the new governor. But, their testimony did not agree and the governor could see no cause for severe punishment. But to stay in the good graces of the Jews, Paul's accusers, Festus asked Paul if he would be willing to go to Jerusalem to be judged. Paul said that he was not willing to do so, that he was standing before Caesar's judgment seat where he ought to be judged. He had done nothing wrong as the governor knew. If he had done wrong and was worthy of death he did not refuse to die. But since the things of which he was accused were untrue, no one could turn him over to his enemies for he was a Roman citizen. He appealed to Caesar. And, since he was a citizen of the Roman Empire his request had to be granted.

A few days later Herod Agrippa, king of Iduma, and Bernice, his beautiful, but wicked sister, came to pay their respects to the new governor. The governor told the king about Paul. The king had heard of the apostle and was anxious to see and hear Paul's defense. So, Paul was brought before the royal group and the king said, "Paul, you are permitted to speak for yourself." So, the apostle stands before the king and the governor, stands before those who have the power to release him from all accusations and he is given the privilege of pleading his own case. What an opportunity! And, what does he make of the opportunity?

He completely ignores his condition as a prisoner, though his very life is at stake, and preaches an impassioned sermon pressing for a decision on the part of the king and governor. He cries, "King Agrippa, do you believe the prophets? I know that you do!" Agrippa said, "Much more of this, Paul, and you will be making me a Christian!" "Ah," returned Paul, "whether it means much more or only a little, I would to God that both you and all who hear me this day might stand where I stand—but without these chains!" What a scene! What a preacher! What passion!

Here, then, is the second time that word "Christian" is used. Paul wrung it from a worldly wise and wicked king. Herod said, "Much more of this, and you will be making a Christian of me!" So, in the second place, a Christian is one who forgets his own safety and welfare in his passionate concern for the spiritual welfare of others.

Methods and techniques vary and are incidental. They change with time and conditions and groups. But, a passionate concern for those who do not know God as he is revealed through Jesus Christ is an essential characteristic of the Christian. That must not be forgotten; it must not be ignored; it must not be watered down; it must not be substituted; it is a necessary ingredient.

Once, it is said, that a man approached Dwight L. Moody, the lay evangelist. The man complained of the methods that Moody used in his revivals. Moody listened sympathetically. When the man had finished the evangelist said that he appreciated the man's criticism. His methods were not always pleasing to himself; he longed to know how to better present Christ to men and women. What methods did the man propose; what techniques did he use? The man said that he had no techniques and he was using no methods for making the gospel known. "Then," said Moody, "I like my methods better than I like yours!" Right. A Christian must bear his witness to those who do not know Christ. It is a necessary characteristic.

A third time that word "Christian" is used in the New Testament. How? It was a time of persecution for the followers of Christ. That is why the First Epistle of Peter was written. The term "Christian" had become a term of contempt. To be branded with it was about the same as being called a thief or a murderer, or some other wrongdoer. The author says, "But take care that none of your number suffers as a murderer, or a thief, a rogue, or spy! If he suffers as a Christian he has nothing to be ashamed of and may glorify God in Christ's name."

Here, then, is a third characteristic of the Christian. The Christian is one who is guilty of no blame as a wrongdoer, but he is true to Christ. If, through being loyal to Christ, punishment and suffering comes his way, he is to convert the experience into a means for bringing glory to God. It is never enough for the Christian to refrain from doing evil; the Christian must convert evil to good. If in doing good, suffering results, he is to take a positive attitude toward it, not just accept it meekly; he is to use the suffering creatively and redemptively. He is to so use it that evil itself becomes a means for doing good.

According to church history the first readers of this instruction took it seriously. Many followed the instruction to the letter! They glorified God through suffering. We have never fully understood just how the followers of Christ conquered the Roman Empire within three hundred years to the extent that they did. No serious and responsible church historian, however, will discount their positive and creative attitude toward suffering. It may well be that more people were won to Christ through the suffering that the Christians *used* than were won by any other

single means. It was how the followers of Christ reacted to
trouble and persecution, how they approached their death and
the death of their loved ones, that the pagan world were quite
unable to explain and were completely unable to ignore. Watch
yourself when trouble comes!

It is said that once a thief was brought before Alexander the
Great to be judged. "What is your name?" asked Alexander.
"My name," responded the thief, "is Alexander." "Then," said
the great Macedonian, "change your name or change your conduct."

> We bear the name of Christian,
> His name and sign we bear;
> O shame, thrice shame upon us,
> To keep him standing there.